Transformation Triumphs

Inspiring Stories of Personal
and Professional Resilience for YOU

Compiled By
Jamie Allen Bishop
Cheryl A. Clark

Transformation Triumphs
Inspiring Stories of Personal and Professional Resilience for YOU

Copyright © 2023

All rights reserved. No part of this book may be reproduced by any mechanical, photographic, or electronic process, or in the form of a phonographic recording; nor may it be stored in a retrieval system, transmitted or otherwise copied for public or private use–other than for "fair use" as brief quotations embodied in articles and reviews–without prior written permission of the publisher.

The authors of this book do not dispense medical advice or prescribe the use of any technique as a form of treatment for physical, emotional, or medical problems without the advice of a physician, either directly or indirectly. Nor is this book intended to provide personalized legal, accounting, financial, or investment advice. Readers are encouraged to seek the counsel of competent professionals with regards to such matters. The intent of the authors is to provide general information to individuals who are taking positive steps in their lives for emotional and spiritual well-being. If you use any of the information in this book for yourself, which is your constitutional right, the authors and the publisher assume no responsibility for your actions.

Published by: Powerful You! Inc. USA
powerfulyoupublishing.com

Library of Congress Control Number: 2023922522

Jamie Allen Bishop and Cheryl A. Clark – First Edition

ISBN: 978-1-959348-21-4

First Edition December 2023

Self-Help/Personal Growth

Dedication

*This book is dedicated to those
who wish to grow internally
so they may find external peace and triumph
in every transformation story.*

Table of Contents

Foreword vii
Introduction xi

1. Lessons From Behind Bars 1
   Cheryl A. Clark

2. Triumphs Through Storytelling .9
   Jamie Allen Bishop

3. Turning Struggle into Strength: Unearthing My Purpose 17
   Jo Mazgay

4. Kindness Changes Everything 25
   Dr. Sabrina Franconeri

5. Dragons It Is, Then! When I Finally Put the Pieces 33
   Together, I Knew What the Answer Was
   Barbara A. Worsley

6. If My Body Quits, Where Am I Going to Live? 43
   Suzy Rawlins

7. Life is Full of Adventure: If You are Willing to Accept It 51
   Diana Cockle

8. From Fired to Fantastic 59
   Wil Becker

Table of Contents

9. Becoming Unshakeable: My Journey from Grief 67
    to Empowerment
      Margaret Dennis

10. Embracing Your Uniqueness 75
      Sharon Loduca

11. Who Am I? 83
      Kellie Haehnel

12. Through the Fear: Cliff-Diving for Beginners 91
      Heaven Sofia

13. A Cause for Pause 99
      Cindy Rose Ferguson

14. Surviving to Thriving in Life! A Transformational Journey. . . 107
      Christine L. Barlet

15. Thriving: One Day at a Time 113
      Jaclyn Kane

About the Authors 119
Acknowledgements & Gratitude 121
About Cheryl. A. Clark 122
About Jamie Allen Bishop 123
About Clare Bennett 125

Foreword

I feel profoundly honored to have been asked to write the foreword for this exceptional book, "Transformational Triumphs." This is a topic I hold very close to my heart.

Change is an inherent part of life, a constant force that shapes our existence. Yet, as human beings, we often find it challenging to willingly embrace change. We may be inspired to change, but more often than not, it's the weight of life's trials that compels us to undergo profound transformations. This moment of necessity is where some of the most remarkable metamorphoses take place.

The topic of transformation is deeply relevant in our present times. Now is an opportune moment to engage in conversations about the changes we are experiencing. Recent global events, such as the pandemic and lockdowns, have pushed us into new places.

During this unique period, people have experienced profound realizations, not only about themselves but also about the world and the essence of life itself. This collective experience serves as a catalyst for change, similar to the hermit archetype, which grows wiser through introspection.

It is within these inner realms that true transformation is conceived, nurtured, and brought to life. Think of it as the chrysalis, the cocoon, where profound changes take place deep inside.

Now, as we move beyond that period of inner reflection, we have sprung forth. These transformations have become visible and we are witnessing the changes that have taken place.

There is profound power and beauty in recognizing that the challenges we encounter in life are not mere obstacles but valuable lessons that guide us toward personal growth and propel us into uncharted territories. It is in the stories we tell and the truths we share that this power and beauty can uplift and inspire others.

Sharing our stories straight from our heart is healing for the person sharing, and for everyone else listening. Within this book the authors authentically share tender parts of their journeys, that have been deeply transformational for them.

As you journey through the chapters that follow, you will encounter a diverse range of individuals who have walked challenging paths, confronting personal and professional adversity that shook the very foundations of their lives. They not only endured but thrived. Their experiences are proof to the power of resilience; it is the power not only to bounce back but to emerge stronger and fuller.

When we experience profound transformation, our pain can become our passion and our passion can become our purpose. There is a reason that life presents these challenges. We are given the opportunity to rise to the challenge.

The creators of this book, Jamie Allen Bishop and Cheryl Clark, are inspirational individuals. Their dedication to this project has imbued it with heart, soul, depth, vulnerability, insights, and self-accountability. They have shown us that true success is rising by lifting others up. Through the sharing of these personal stories, healing takes place, and we can truly believe that yes, transformation IS possible.

As you read these personal stories, you may find aspects of your own heartache mirrored within them for these are universal human experiences. As painful as it may be, emotional pain does serve a

Foreword

purpose and does have the ability to break our hearts open. You will read about the themes of well-being and self-love echoed through these pages, illustrating that love is healing, and healing is real.

"Transformation Triumphs" is a relatable collection of our life's narratives. These stories will resonate with you, as you will see your own journey reflected in the struggles and successes of these remarkable individuals. They are more than just stories of resilience; they are blueprints for embracing change, overcoming adversity, and emerging victorious.

Each narrative demonstrates that resilience is available to us all, for it is in fact an innate quality of humanity. When nurtured and developed, it becomes a powerful tool to navigate life's most challenging moments.

"Transformation Triumphs" shines as a beacon of hope, reminding us that we all possess remarkable resilience. Whether you are navigating personal crises, professional setbacks, or simply seeking personal growth, this book offers insights and inspiration to guide your journey. May the stories contained within these pages be that reminder to us all of the potential that resides within each one of us.

With an open heart and an eager spirit, I invite you to embark on this journey of self-reflection through the pages of "Transformation Triumphs." As you read, may you find inspiration, wisdom, and the unwavering belief that, no matter the challenges life presents, you hold the power to triumph in your own transformation.

With love,
Clare Bennett
Temple Divine
Scotland, UK

Introduction

They say, "It takes a village."
We agree!
In our personal and professional lives, transformation is a word to represent a release of what no longer serves us...a change...a renewal. An experience that provided an opportunity for growth and expansion. Two core elements that aid in this process are:

> PERSEVERANCE: The determination to move beyond life's challenges... the tenacity to do whatever it takes... the grit to climb that hill, despite the fear or the unknown, in order to achieve your vision and/or desired goal.

> SUPPORT: Exploring the possibilities through educating ourselves by reading/research. Having the foresight to reach out to our community for aid, encouragement, or mentorship. Knowing that We NEVER get there alone.

We are honored to share this group of stories as the Transformation Triumphs of our authors. Each author shares their personal story of how they achieved transformation in their own lives. May their journey inspire YOU to reach and achieve YOUR own transformation.

We are grateful for your interest in Transformation Triumphs and wish you success in all your future endeavors. Your time is NOW!

TRANSFORMATION TRIUMPHS

Allow these Stories to Be Your Inspiration

CHAPTER 1
Lessons From Behind Bars
Cheryl A. Clark

Does carbon dioxide poisoning hurt?
How long before you pass from carbon dioxide inhalation?
How long can a car idle with a quarter tank of gas?
What are the chances of living when one is exposed to carbon dioxide?
How many sleeping pills do you need to take before you die in your sleep?

All the above can be found in my Google search history. There are others here and there about train impacts, though they were always tainted by the thoughts that some poor innocent train driver would be shattered thinking they had taken a life and not realizing that the life they took was well-lived and the person (meaning me) simply wanted out on a good note.

Though it may be hard to believe, I can be a bit of a Pollyanna. My exit was always painted in my mind as coming after a life well-lived, with humans impacted positively and amazing experiences and memories collected. It would happen when it was, in my eyes, time to depart.

Let me share how my desire to leave this world would land me behind bars for two hundred ninety-five days. Yes, imagine—wanting to die, only to be put in handcuffs and removed from what you knew to be home. There is a whole conversation we could have around systems and how ill-equipped they are to "deal" with so many human factors, but I won't go into that here.

On September 7, 2017, I wrote a beautiful Facebook post about my life, some of the amazing experiences and great friendships I've had. More importantly, I wrote about how over the past thirteen months I had come to love in a way I had never believed possible, thanks to a newborn baby I was fostering while her mother worked to get clean from opiates. The post concluded with, "I won't commit suicide after all, because no one could properly tell 'Pohpoh' (my nickname for the baby) how much I love her."

Though I had clearly stated I would not do anything to myself, my post, like so many others, were skimmed and misconstrued. The takeaway: Cheryl is suicidal. (Truthfully, I was "ish," however I had talked myself out of it, for that moment, at least.)

I don't blame my friends for their fear. A few even called in "well checks" for me, and though I'm grateful and know they were only doing what they knew to do at the time, those "well checks" definitely sent me into a tailspin.

The rap at the door, the peek through the peep hole, and seeing three officers confused me. I had no idea they were there for me! When I opened the door, I was asked to identify myself and step outside. When I did, I was asked if I was okay, to which I of course responded with a "YES! I am good!"

One thing led to another rather quickly.

Before I knew it, I was asked to come with them for a record check. Coming with them involved handcuffs, a backseat of a police car and being put into a cell until paperwork could be sorted, understood, and dealt with. Coming with them would be the last time I would see my home, my material possessions, the baby I

Chapter 1
Lessons From Behind Bars

had come to love. Coming with them would mean no contact with friends for two hundred ninety-five days. Coming with them…led me to this…

I had never been in handcuffs before.

I had never had any run-in with the law.

I had never had an anxiety attack before either. Let me tell you, putting a five-foot, ten-inch gal who weighed close to two hundred pounds at the time into a police car is no easy task. Now, when I watch TV shows about officers and detainment, those limber humans who can kick and scream and wiggle around in those backseats have my utmost respect. It took everything in me to fill my lungs in those moments to keep sitting up straight, let alone the knee bruises I was getting and cuff marks from my back pushed into the seat with my hands/arms in between.

The Mesa, Arizona police station was my first stop.

Then the famous 4th Avenue Jail was my next stop. This was where I was asked my citizenship, proof of my stay in the United States and when I knew I was in fact going to struggle with the Immigration department.

After a court date was set to sort out the paperwork, I was released on my own recognizance. A second later, however, just as one set of cuffs came off, another set went on. That second set belonged to United States Immigration Officers.

Oh, the stories I could write about 4th Avenue Jail. The stories I could write about those struggling with addiction and how the jail scene was like a Girl Scouts meeting—they all knew one another in some fashion or another, whether personally, or by association or even by street corner. I was completely out of my element; I watched and listened without moving a muscle. It was my first taste of knowing what a privileged life I had.

Here's a snapshot of my journey with the American penal system: Police car to the Mesa Police Department, the 4th Avenue Jail, Phoenix Immigration Office, Florence Detainment Center, Phoenix Immigration office, and the Eloy Detainment Center—all within ninety-six hours. In November, I went from Eloy Detainment Center to 4th Avenue Jail, to Estrella Jail, to Phoenix Immigration office, to Florence Detainment Center and back to Eloy Detainment Center. In June of 2018 I was shifted from Eloy Detainment Center to Albany, New York, and eventually released at the Niagara Canadian Border back into Canada.

Jail/detainment is like being immersed in a new country for the first time. There is a whole new lingo and a whole new set of "laws" and "rules," but the governing body is not made up of those elected or paid to be there, but your fellow detainees. Sure, there are some powers afforded to those employed by these places, but for the most part the rules and laws and expectations are absolutely set by those in the same clothing and uniform as I was wearing.

Kites—What is a kite? Lockdown—what does that mean? Shakedown—What is this, a dance move? Pat down—Why? What is worth stealing in these places? Now take into account that eighty-five percent of the people in Eloy were Hispanic, only ten percent of them bilingual, and you can see that for sure I was a minority, not only in terms of language and skin tones, but life experience.

But, oh, what I learned, and can even say accomplished. Do not tell me white privilege doesn't exist, because I've lived it. I was addressed differently by the guards; I was afforded privileges some never would see—all because of my skin color and language.

I also learned a great deal about what is valued depending on where we are in the world. For example, in the United States, book education is more valued by those in power than "street

Chapter 1
Lessons From Behind Bars

knowledge" or farming. I have always had paper, pens, and scissors at my disposal. If I decided to make something, I had the tools to craft it. Without those tools, however, I was "powerless." Many of the women from Guatemala and other South American countries, however, had learned to use their hands and whatever items were readily available to them. Give one of them a ramen noodle package and in no time she would fold it up, heat water to work it and then would present an amazing necklace, bracelet, or bookmark!

We were in the United States—holding them to "standards" they weren't aware of, standards they didn't understand. This was one of the biggest lessons I learned while detained. We spoke to them in English—they didn't understand. We used words that their informal or "street" knowledge may have never taught them. We used terms they didn't know. Expected their routines for hygiene, eating, dressing, sleeping to be like ours. Yet, when I paused long enough to learn about them and hear their stories, I realized these ladies knew a passion I would possibly never experience…a passion for living, working, and community. They knew a resilience beyond my comprehension. They knew a hope I could not grasp.

I met ladies who'd had their feet torched so they could not run from those abusing them. I met ladies who'd lost family members to cartels, gangs, and corrupt leaders. I met ladies who could share story after story of what you and I would consider torture, abuse, and hardships. Yet—they called it life. I met ladies who were willing to walk thousands of miles looking for hope and believing it existed, regardless of what they knew and had experienced.

One planet, one team.

I met ladies who smiled and were grateful for running water. I met ladies who were excited to have a TV and microwave available. I met ladies who rallied around one struggling and believed in community. All of the above are among what I would call the "fresh border-crossers."

Then there are the stories of those who, like me, had been in the United States for years upon years, then found themselves detained thinking life as they knew it was over. Many knew of no other country, having been brought over to the U.S. as infants, and were facing deportation—and separation from their families, homes and loved ones—because of a lack of papers.

I, at least, knew I was going to be returned to a safe country. Some were being sent to war-torn Congo, others to the depths of Mexico, others back to India to be placed in submissive experiences.

These ladies were often there because of a "call" or a "poor choice"—meaning they called the police for help during a domestic violence situation and were detained. In my case, it was that Facebook post saying I was tired and had a great life and was time to exit led me to being there. Yes, I was "good enough" to foster a newborn and run a business all those years, but apparently I did not meet the requirement to stay in my home.

What were my biggest lessons?

Community is where you are and is ALWAYS buildable. Those who have been detained remain connected and there for one another, even after their release. Some of you may call this a trauma bond (and rightfully so); regardless, it's a bond that sustains, supports, uplifts, and is deeper than most will ever experience (or allow themselves to experience, for don't we all go into friendships somewhat guarded?)

You adapt. The goal of steak on the barbeque every night shifted to praying for boiled eggs in the morning! You learn

Chapter 1
Lessons From Behind Bars

to adapt and set your sights on what is attainable and within your reach. You learn to cheer for seemingly small victories when the large ones can't be found. You adapt.

Energy is contagious. That "you can do it" attitude changed my living experience behind bars. Being an encourager brought me encouragement.

Your voice matters. Many feared the authorities and were taught to respect it at all costs and all times. Empowering advocacy for oneself was a big part of my journey. We (in North America) have a voice and we use it. Teaching others that it was okay to question, it was okay to say no, it was okay to ask, and it was okay to pause, was eye-opening.

Holding people to what you know is not fair. Asking the ladies for medical records to prove their torture, asking mothers for copies of their children's birth certificates to prove the children were theirs, asking ladies for proof of housing and travel…you get the picture. We were expecting and asking them for things they simply could not produce, didn't have, and didn't understand. Meet people where they are at!

See the journey! Often, we see a choice, a decision, one step of where someone is at and what they have "done." We base perceptions on this moment, even judgments. There are many steps that led them to that moment! There are many steps taken since that moment as well. See the journey, not just that step. We see the slip, the stumble; we don't understand it because we are not in their shoes and yet we focus on it and hold them there in our minds. Now, I am not advocating illegal entry whatsoever; however, I am saying understand the journey and help rather than judge.

Oh, the book inside of me…one day. All of this may have you wondering where I am today! I am in Ontario, Canada. I have reconnected with many of my amazing American friends and, thanks to my detainment, I also now have friends pretty much worldwide. It is my hope to get to Mexico soon to hug on those who shared in this experience with me! "We are in it together" holds new meaning for many of us and rings so true! Time, distance, country, language, education, skin tone—they are all just excuses for lack of unity. When you get rid of the excuses, what do you find?

Same planet, same team.

ABOUT THE AUTHOR: Cheryl Clark is a speaker, an author, a trainer, and a business growth specialist; however, she prefers such titles as human, hugger, and friend. Cheryl has been blessed to speak in Vegas, Arizona, Colorado, California, and, most recently, Ontario, Canada. Personal and professional connecting strategies have become her passion. Cheryl is known for her humanitarian nature, especially after her experiences during a ten-month detainment in an immigration camp in the United States. She speaks on behalf of those needing a voice, her favorite line being, "Led me to this…"

Cheryl A. Clark
LED ME TO THIS
ledmetothis.com
mystory@ledmetothis.com
facebook.com/ledmetothis

CHAPTER 2

Triumphs Through Storytelling

Jamie Allen Bishop

I like movies...and books, and theater, and sitcoms. Really, it's storytelling that I love. Storytelling is a gift not everyone has but most can appreciate. There is a method to the madness that makes storytelling relatable, and our stories are what make up our lives. They also bridge the gap between your story and mine, encouraging us to relate to each other at a soul level, embrace our differences, and see the beauty in being similarly unique.

The question is, what happens to our lives when we allow ourselves to relate to a story or to be the storyteller?

Let's take movies, for example. When you go behind the scenes of these productions, the artistry involved in the camera angle, the sound score, and the lighting choices all combine to make (or break) a movie's success. In addition, the business aspects of these undertakings are nothing short of miraculous—determining which stories to tell, which actor might represent them best, and how much to invest in the production. It's a gamble...every step of the process.

What I cherish about movies, however, is being at the theater. It's the combination of the film, the chairs, the food, the smells, the audience, the emotion, the reactions, the community, etcetera. Watching a movie in the theater is a magical experience, my little slice of heaven.

> *"Life is what you make of it, friend.*
> *If it doesn't fit, you make alterations."*
> Stella (Linda Hunt) Silverado (1985)

Movies are storytelling in action. We can relate to the characters. We get involved in the plot. We are typically led on a rollercoaster ride of emotions and reactions—all in a couple of hours.

This brings me to another thing I love about storytelling. Each story is neat, tidy, and complete. There's a beginning (what s/he thought s/he wanted), a middle (the part where s/he overcomes obstacles), and an end (when s/he realizes this new experience is what s/he wanted all along). Storytelling can settle our worries and engage our empathy in ways that real life sometimes can't. No matter how we react to the story's emotional impact, we typically end up leaving the theater a little changed, a little better for the experience. That neat and tidy bow makes us feel like maybe life isn't that complicated after all.

Is life that simple? Do the stories we tell ourselves make (or break) our lives?

> *"You don't want to be in love.*
> *You want to be in love in a movie!"*
> ~ Becky (Rosie O'Donnell) in Sleepless in Seattle (1993)

Movies have a ridiculous number of ups and downs, and twists and turns. Real-life stories do too, but when moments don't wrap up as easily or neatly as they do in the movies, we are left with parts of our soul confused, torn, and tattered. Those so-called broken pieces might be blowing in the wind like the embers of a fire for years, wreaking havoc on our lives and the lives of those we love. Real life can leave us open to the harsh elements of disappointment and longing, lacking faith, fearful of the future, or—even worse—

Chapter 2
Triumphs Through Storytelling

doubting ourselves.

> *"Some people can't believe in themselves*
> *until someone else believes in them first."*
> ~ *Sean Maguire (Robin Williams) in Good Will Hunting (1997)*

When I was twenty-nine, living in Atlanta, Georgia, I came to the horrible realization that we are taught subconsciously through movie storytelling that closure is supposed to wrap up in moments rather than in lifetimes. I was in the middle of an amicable divorce when it dawned on me that because of this false idea about closure I struggled to understand what went wrong and why there were no easy answers. I knew it was the end of one thing and the beginning of something else, but I couldn't understand why it was taking so long to emotionally recover. Without that neat and tidy bow to wrap up the story, how was I supposed to know when I experienced a transformation or a triumph?

> *"My mother once told me that bad news*
> *is just good news in disguise."*
> ~ *Sid the Sloth (John Leguizamo) in Ice Age,*
> *Continental Drift (2012)*

Struggles are only part of the story, not the whole story. To recognize my own transformations and triumphs, I take a logical approach by evaluating where I have been, where I am currently, and where I am going. With this as my guide, it's easier to allow my emotions to find the successes this lifetime has shown me.

Writing things down can help us consider the storyline trifecta of transformation—the beginning, the middle, and the end. When we write, it gives us a chance to view our lives and plan for something beyond today.

> *"Don't ever let someone tell you (that) you can't do*
> *something. Not even me. ...You want something, go get it.*

Transformation Triumphs

> *Period. All right?"*
> ~ Chris Gardner (Will Smith) in
> The Pursuit of Happyness (2006)

One of my most significant transformation triumph stories was in 2007. It was the profound moment I realized I was deeply healed at a soul level. I could tell you hundreds, if not thousands, of similar stories, but this is the one that came to me when I sat down to write this chapter.

Point of view: I was in a Master's of Art Education program at one university when I found myself also taking a Master Toe Reader Certification course at a nearby college. Some family members were discussing (behind my back) the need for an intervention. They were very concerned about me, about who I was listening to, and about what my future held, especially since I was the primary caregiver to my young and impressionable toddler. From their perspective, I had reckless devotion to people and teachings that were "weird," and they weren't about to stand by without doing something about it.

> *"The only way that we can measure the significance of our own lives is by valuing the lives of others."*
> ~ David Gale (Kevin Spacey) in The Life of David Gale (2003)

I happened across their message exchange—weeks in the making—and I was profoundly hurt by the words I read.

It's funny what our brain does when we read something. Somehow, reading can make us believe things without question. Reading allows our imagination to come to life, and we often take the words as truth. Something in written form can be perceived as heart-warming or heart-wrenching, depending on the writer's state of mind when it is written, but also depending on our own state of mind when we read it.

Upon reflection of what I had read, these words from *The Course*

Chapter 2
Triumphs Through Storytelling

in Miracles washed over my soul and echoed in my head, *"There are only two emotions: love and fear. Only love exists."*

Wow! I had come across this belief years earlier, but I hadn't examined it until I started taking the toe reading courses. This concept instantly calmed me. Hurt? Yes! Angry? Yes! But why? What was the fear behind my reaction?

My biggest fear was losing my kid, the one pure and true love of my life. What if they decided I was crazy, had me committed to a psych ward, and took my baby from me? What if that is what was best for her? What if my husband left me? What would happen to us? What would happen to me?

I was angry. I felt judged. Without even talking to me about what I was learning, these people who are supposed to be my support system had decided what was best for me. They determined I was being led down the path of (self?) destruction. They decided without even asking me to tell them about it.

> *"People say a lot of things in anger.*
> *It is our choice whether or not to listen."*
> ~ Mrs. Potts (Emma Thompson) in Beauty and the Beast (2017)

My former reaction—a fear-based one—might have been from anger, defense, or resentment, i.e.: "How dare you talk about me behind my back! Who do you think you are? You don't know what you're talking about! F* you!"

Thankfully, it didn't take more than five minutes for that calm feeling to take root. I took a few deep breaths, released my fear, and responded to them from this perspective: "Message received. I appreciate that you care about me. Thank you. If it makes you uncomfortable, I won't talk about my beliefs in front of you anymore. I love you."

Guess what happened?

Yep, they backed down. Backpedaled. Apologized profusely. Recognized their conversation was out of line and not something either of them would have said to my face. They understood that their discussion was wrong. From my firm stance of knowing who I was (love) and what they were conveying in their conversation (fear), my heart-centered reaction washed away their concerns along with my own.

What I learned through our exchange was that when we take an extra close look at what we might initially perceive as a threat or a disappointment or a challenge, we realize that love is all that truly exists. Everything else is made up in the story we tell ourselves. We are in control of shifting the story from a place of fear to a place of love. When we do, miracles happen.

Since that communication, my relationship with these family members has changed for the better. There weren't many questions about my beliefs or about what kind of witchery is involved in toe reading (none), and nobody ever asked why my reaction was so different from what it used to be (my new focus on love), but our relationship with each other has developed a level of respect that wasn't there before this interaction. Because of the dramatic shift in these relationships, my awareness was one of transformation. It was a triumph for me, and I hope for my family members, too.

"Life is long. It'd be pretty boring if we had to stay
the same version of ourselves the whole time."
Heidi (Kate Bosworth) in Along for the Ride (2022)

It took me a while to realize that this one story has dynamically changed all the stories that followed it, and even some of the stories that happened before it. When we review the stories we tell ourselves, and we look at them through a lens of love rather than a lens of fear, some of the rotten things our loved ones have done to us don't seem

Chapter 2
Triumphs Through Storytelling

as devastating, or the lessons learned are more powerful than the pain. Experiencing a soul-altering story is about being aware of the journey and about shifting our focus to love. The love lens fosters our becoming the best version of ourselves and supports our loved ones in being the best version of themselves too.

When we shift our perspective, we can shift the stories of our lives. When we decide to have a firm conviction of who we are, and we take a solid stance in seeing the love in every story, we become the writers of our lives. We become the s/hero of our own tale.

> *"Iris, in the movies, we have leading ladies, and we have the best friend. You, I can tell, are a leading lady, but for some reason, you're behaving like the best friend."*
> *~ Arthur Abbot (Eli Wallach) in The Holiday (2006)*

Unwavering confidence is a learned characteristic, one that we are not always taught as children. Even as adults, there is nothing quite like a family's judgmental comment that can rattle our soul. When that happens to me, I know there is still work *I* need to do. There is still releasing *I* must allow and forgiveness *I* desire to embrace. Here's why it's my issue: the words or actions of another cannot harm a truly healed heart.

> *"Dreams make good stories, but everything important happens while we're awake."*
> *~ Duncan Idaho (Jason Momoa) in Dune (2021)*

Each story we wrap up with that neat and tidy bow shifts our soul toward peace and joy, which is what I believe makes a successful life. I pray for everyone to be enlightened to the slice of heaven that is a movie-going experience, and I hope that each of us can see the stories in our lives a little clearer when we see them through the lens of love. It might take years, possibly decades, maybe even lifetimes, to get to a place where our challenges can be seen as transformation triumphs. We are the storytellers of our own lives. It is up to each of us to view our story as a triumph worth telling.

ABOUT THE AUTHOR: Jamie Allen Bishop is an international bestselling author and speaker dedicated to transforming struggling entrepreneurs into thriving success stories through the power of social media. With a track record of excellence, she has helped 100% of her clients achieve growth and traction in their businesses. Jamie's expertise lies in guiding entrepreneurs to cultivate a growth mindset, master time management on social media platforms, build strong support networks, and chart their path to prosperity. Her laser coaching program unlocks the secrets to building a rock-solid foundation for launching a positive impact in the world.

Jamie Allen Bishop, MA
Mindset Coach for New Entrepreneurs
JamieAllenBishop.com
Jamie@JamieAllenBishop.com
#JamieAllenBishop

CHAPTER 3

Turning Struggle into Strength
Unearthing My Purpose
Jo Mazgay

Life is hard—we can all agree on that, right?

Daily stresses overwhelm us without the right mindset to keep us moving forward. I, for one, am honestly getting tired of the narrative that we should "just think positive."

I am a ray of fucking sunshine, I work damn hard to keep that mindset, but again I ask: can we all agree that it gets exhausting? I have done the work, I have done so much work, and yet…I still feel the shadows creep in. I still get overwhelmed, I still cry, I have doubt and self-sabotage like you. Imposter syndrome is a real thing.

What you all don't see behind my happy and motivational posts, which I truly and authentically believe in, is the messy kitchen, piles of laundry, and real-life situations that I deal with, the same as you do.

I am a single mom to four kids, and, at forty-eight, pursuing my first university degree. I have no immediate family around me. My life is not easy. I live with anxiety, depression, ADHD, and crippling social anxiety—and my kids all have varying degrees of the same. It takes work, so much work, to stay positive, to stay on this side of life. My mindset keeps me going, as do various medications and a great social network—when I have the ability to reach out. If you know anxiety, you know how scary a phone call can be. There are times when I would have rather eaten glass than answer a phone call. I have managed my anxiety well for years now, and I have not had a full-blown anxiety attack in over seven years. I still don't answer phone calls from unknown numbers, though.

This past summer hit me hard.

My happy place is in nature. This is where I feel grounded, this is where I breathe deeper, this is where I feel peace in my heart. I love the sounds, the loons and frogs, kids laughing, fires crackling, and water—*my gawd*, I love being by the water. This is where I bring my kids to disconnect, to be kids and play; we all sleep differently after being outdoors all day. Now, my children live a much different life with their father. And that's okay. I believe that experiencing both my world and his life in the city will bring them balance and the choice as to how they want to live. Full disclosure: the differences between the two sometimes trigger Imposter Syndrome around what I can provide for them as a parent. Example: this past summer, he planned a European holiday for them—two weeks exploring Italy and France. I took them camping. See what I mean?

Last spring, when I went to open my trailer, I found it had leaked during the winter. We get big storms out by the lake, and I love them. I love feeling the energy of a furious summer storm coming in, the power of that thunder and lightning, but I do not enjoy the rainwater leaking through my walls!

I soon discovered the cause of the leak was in the tip-out (an expandable room for an RV). The weather stripping was done and it was on me to figure out how to fix it. I googled, YouTubed, and

Chapter 3
Turning Struggle into Strength

Yahooed, trying to find a solution I could put together on my own, on a single-mom budget. Just keeping this place—a fifteen-year-old RV by a quiet lake—was my budget.

It's not fancy, but it's mine. It's not Europe, but I'm trying.

And it's leaking.

I put on my big girl panties (Who am I kidding? I am far more powerful commando in ass-kicker boots, but that's another book!) and I started peeling away the rotting weather striping. I had gotten RV sealing tape on Amazon. To every seasoned camper who just read that and rolled their eyes, you're right, and it didn't work. Thankfully, being a seasonal site in a family campground, the sense of community is incredible here. My friend Bill approached, shook his head, and said, "Stop doing this, caulk it." Then I got the wonderful fatherly tutorial on caulking that I should have gotten at twenty, but back then I was too busy chasing boys to listen anyway.

Grateful for the advice, I wadded up the ridiculous RV tape, which was more stuck to me than my trailer, and threw that aside. As I began caulking, I could hear the thunder rumbling in the distance. A storm was coming, but my tip-out was now bare to the elements, so I had to finish the job.

I believe in thinking smarter not harder, so I asked myself what would be the most efficient way to get this job done properly. I got rid of the ladder, put the tip-out halfway in, and backed my truck up parallel to the RV so I could reach where I needed to be without going up and down a ladder.

Feeling good about this solution, I started caulking. This might be a good time to point out that I am handy-ish...meaning I can figure out a lot with common sense. Then again, I had never caulked a trailer before. I was trying to move quickly, the thunder boomed louder, the wind was picking up, the birds were not singing, this storm was getting closer. I found my breath, I focused my mindset. *I can do hard things*, I thought. *I am doing this so I can give my kids this beautiful experience*—all the while listening to them talk about how excited they were to go to Italy. The Imposter syndrome rears its ugly head.

I can do hard things.

Fat raindrops begin, the kind that make their own splash as they hit your skin. I am so close to being done, just a few more inches, then it will be dry, safe from the elements. Thunder cracks overhead, and all I have time to do is pull the tarp over the tip-out, jump off the truck, and go inside. I am hot, sweating, and exhausted, but I can do hard things. I caulked my own tip-out, I am showing my kids that we can do things, and how great it feels to have that sense of accomplishment. Except the rain is pouring in through the tip-out. Pouring. I feel defeat heavy in my chest, and the overwhelm takes over.

Why do I even try?

Kids don't want to go camping, frogs aren't exciting anymore. My teenager scoffs at the lack of Wi-Fi and is sooooooo booooooored. They want trips to Europe that they can post on social media. They want to go shopping in boutiques and taste real Italian gelato, and I took them camping in an old, leaky RV. Now the clouds in my mind are getting darker. I'm a terrible mom. Who do I think I am to think I can maintain this alone? I'm alone. I don't have a partner, my family is nowhere near, and they would probably tell me the same. I cannot do this alone. I cannot caulk a thirty-foot trailer and have it work right before a storm—how dumb am I? Now, I am crying, using all the towels, bedding, everything that is dry, to

Chapter 3
Turning Struggle into Strength

try and keep the water from getting into the walls; *oh, gawd,* I am about to expose my kids to black mold if this can't be contained. My kids are watching me completely bewildered, ready to pack up and go home, because I failed. The storm finally ends, as they all do, and feeling completely defeated, I muster everything I have to go see the outside...what did I do so wrong? My neighbor calmly and cautiously approaches the hot mess that I am and simply says, "It seems you have a problem here." I nod and state the obvious: "Yes, it's still leaking." He smiles, and says, "Well, open or close it, but don't leave it halfway out, or the water will come in." *Will come in?* Niagara Falls had just passed through my sanctuary. Everything is ruined; I failed and I cannot do hard things. I'm crying again. Fuck, I hate being weak, vulnerable, alone.

Wait, what? Open the tip-out the rest of the way?

The storm came, and I jumped off my truck and pulled the tarp over. I did not reopen my tip-out. I left it halfway out in my rush to get out of the storm.

I went inside, opened the tip-out fully, and all the water went out with it. Holy shit.

That is how an anxious mind works. I can go from zero to worst-case scenario faster than anyone, and when you are in it, you cannot stop it. That's why I do the work. Telling someone in an anxiety attack to breathe is like telling an angry mom to calm down...Please don't do that!

So now it's drier.

All my towels, bedding, soaked...Kids, still don't really care. I had so much to clean up, and they all wanted to be fed. Didn't you have breakfast? Lunch? Now you want dinner too? I am trying to provide a sanctuary here!!!

I was still under a dark cloud, but it was Canada Day—and my son Declyn's eleventh birthday. He spent it camping in the rain, riding his bike through puddles, best day ever. That's eleven—gawd, I love eleven! Until recently, Declyn believed the Canada Day fireworks were for his birthday. A bit grandiose, I know, but so magical in the eyes of a child.

In honor of the holiday, our park puts on fireworks over the lake, and they do a really great job, but I was not in the space to people. My friend came by and asked if I was coming to the beach to watch, but no, I just wanted to pout. She told me she had a chair for me if I changed my mind. *Thank you, Brandy.* Five minutes later, Ralph showed up. "Jo, let's go," he said, "We are about to start." I try to say no, but he won't hear it. They had something planned that I needed to see. I grudgingly got up, found Brandy, and we went down to watch the fireworks. Pouting but present is the best I can do today. Then Ralph called Declyn up, front and center.

"I hear it's your birthday," Ralph said, and Declyn beamed—the biggest eleven-year-old smile you have ever seen. One hundred campers sang Happy Birthday to my son. I'm already about to cry. Then Ralph said, "Well, eleven, that is a pretty big deal. How do you feel?" Declyn was so happy in that moment; he was eleven and all these people were celebrating him. Not Canada Day, but him, and that is pretty amazing.

Ralph then told Declyn what an important member of the community he was—and since turning eleven was such a big deal, would he like to set off the first firework? I didn't think my son's smile could get any bigger, but it did. He was beaming. The crowd was cheering for him and his friends were looking on in amazement as the gentlemen who ran the event every year called him over, told

Chapter 3
Turning Struggle into Strength

him where to stand, and how to safely ignite the firework. My boy did not hesitate. Boom! The sky exploded, and I could not stop crying.

Ralph came over to me and said, "Italy won't give him *that*."

Suddenly, the leaking trailer doesn't define this day. Community does. Love does. Eleven does. Remembering why we do this, is right in front of me.

Doing hard things is so much more rewarding when there is a why at the end. In that moment, I looked around at this crowd of mostly strangers (because, let's face it… social anxiety) and I saw a community that rallied for my son. I felt community. I knew Declyn would remember this moment for the rest of his life.

Why did I bust my ass to maintain a trailer?

Why did I drive so far out of the city?

Why do I bring my kids here when they want trips to Europe and Wi-Fi?

Community.

Feeling a part of a community, even from my own seclusion, wherein I only talk to five other campers, is a powerful feeling. It is that feeling of inclusion and genuine caring that forms the basis of all my programs for women.

That's my why.

As you read this, my hope is you begin to think about yours.

What is your why? Your purpose?

We are not here to eat, sleep, work, and pay bills.

We are here to form connections, create change, and experience life.

When you determine your why, everything—even the hard things—has purpose, and having purpose allows us to see the reward of our work. The why is the reward at the end. The why is what allows us to bring our core beliefs into our work. Even caulking a trailer as a thunderstorm looms overhead has purpose. It gives me back a feeling of community, some peace in nature, and allows me to provide my children a view of the world that will inspire them to choose how they want to live.

That is my why.

ABOUT THE AUTHOR: Jo Mazgay is a motivational speaker and creator of platforms, events, and workshops for women that facilitate the release of shame and loneliness, support mental wellness, and foster community. *Transformation Triumphs* is Jo's second book project, following the successful *Conscious Transformation* (2021). Both are preludes to her upcoming book about experiencing and embracing her feminine, unapologetically. Jo teaches within her own company, Embraced Hearts Community and Big Brothers Big Sisters; she is also a Core Leader with Soul Full Camps Ontario. She has been featured in numerous Canadian magazines as a leader in embodying The Divine Feminine and co-hosts the weekly show *Keep It Raw, Keep It Real* on Otunes radio.

Jo Mazgay
JoMazgay.com
Cofounder of EmbracedHeartsCommunity.com
Follow @Jo_Mazgay or #JoMazgay to explore her offerings

CHAPTER 4

Kindness Changes Everything

Dr. Sabrina Franconeri

I once had a very different life. I had a teaching career filled with ups and downs. I cried on my first day on the job, testified in juvenile court over a student crime, and conquered a rumor mill that put the dirtiest tabloids to shame. I saw students exceed their potential and met some wonderful people. I had a difficult engagement, beautiful wedding, lukewarm honeymoon, and terrible marriage. I had an amazing circle of family and friends who were alienated because of my choice in a spouse. An inevitable, epic divorce followed, with lows of financial worries and highs of learning what I require in an intimate partner. During it all, I found a career that fed and empowered me, but developed a natural armor because I was hardened by reality. I struggled when asked to bring my whole and authentic self to work. I saw employers talk the talk, but not walk the walk. I questioned how to truly be me in environments where I didn't feel safe.

I am a product of my environment and spent the bulk of my career priding myself on my abilities to learn fast, work faster, and, above all, strive for the unattainable concept of perfection. I have been bullied, broken, and pushed to the limit by bosses, colleagues, significant others, friends, and, worst of all, myself. I thought I had to become a certain person to earn respect, not realizing that I allowed Imposter Syndrome to swallow me alive. I was afraid to reveal a glimpse behind the curtain. What I did not know at the time was that each reveal contributed to a transformational realization: kind people are successful people.

In today's tumultuous society, we often see less kindness when we really need more. Events contribute to human behavior, but there are other factors to consider. Kind people can appear unintelligent, timid, or weak. Kindness can also be a sign of introversion, a personality type seen as "bad" in many industries. But kindness shows emotional intelligence and helps form mutually beneficial relationships. ***Kindness changes everything.***

Typos and Accusations

I was hired by a large law firm in a newly created professional development position. I'd worked with several lawyers during my teaching stints, so I had some knowledge about the personalities, but not much else. I did not know what it was like to work in an office since I was always in the classroom. I was also the only non-lawyer on the new team, but that did not scare me. I was excited to hit the ground running!

Right away, it seemed like a lot of great things were happening that I was not part of. I know now that I was "paying my dues," but at twenty-six, dues was a foreign concept. I learned that lawyers were laser-focused on certain details but lacked emotional intelligence. My boss would approach me with an accusatory tone for things such as typos or unclear information. Some days, it felt like I was hired to be her personal whipping post. My colleagues didn't take time to get to know me. Everything seemed to be my fault, and when it came time for my first performance review I was surprised that I

Chapter 4
Kindness Changes Everything

was not fired. My boss was shocked when I told her this, and even said, "We never meant to give you that impression!" I eventually enjoyed friendships, raises, successes, and a promotion but still received the same tonality and criticism without warning or context. Following the cues, I started treating people the way I was being treated. This model seemed to make others credible and successful, and I wanted that so much.

Things came full circle in what was to be my final performance review. It was glowing, but I was told that I needed to be more considerate of people's feelings when I communicated. I was livid for being penalized for learned behavior. I argued back with venom, expressing that this happened over time because of the way I was treated. As it turned out, they liked my style and personality! I helped balance out the energy on the team, and to be truly successful in the role I needed to bring my "whole and authentic self." The fact that they couldn't communicate this upfront proves that lawyers need better training on emotional intelligence. The real me was valued and ***kindness changed everything***.

The Monster

I eventually changed jobs and cities, but not industries. A better title and higher salary gave me the chance to truly start over after my divorce. But I was not prepared for the new environment—one in which multiple eyes and ears were focused on me. I'd left a smaller city where everyone knew your business, so I was surprised to see this elsewhere. I inherited a lot of problems that had not been properly dealt with, a lack of internal infrastructure, a difficult department chair, and a generation gap in my team. The group of lawyers had even less emotional intelligence than my original batch, so I was stepping onto an enormous battlefield.

Internal politics challenged me to my core. There were many "lifers," people who joined with cemented relationships, and many rounds of the "telephone game." At one point I felt like I was bugged, because no matter what type of conversation I had or what I did on the outside, it made it back inside. My role evolved into the opposite of what I was originally sold, making me resentful. The resentment became frustration, which evolved into anger. I did not know who to trust and hated the work. Severe anxiety would kick in each morning as I approached my metro stop. My attitude was terrible—I had become a monster.

Eventually, I was confronted about that attitude. It was a raw, deep, and painful conversation in which I felt exposed and vulnerable. It created tension that lasted for months. I regretted my transparency, but focused on what I could control: myself. It takes a lot of energy to be constantly angry, and I was relieved to let some of the anger subside. I grew more positive about my employment situation and, as my attitude improved, so did my options, gradually setting me up to take a new professional step. I did not know it then, but ***kindness changed everything.***

Expectations, Terminations and a Pandemic…Oh My!

I left the legal industry for a role in a global environment that was one hundred percent focused on learning and development. I wanted it that way. Overall, I fit, gaining amazing experience through travel, and managing a diverse team across the globe. I also inherited newly hidden problems: some unrealistic expectations, stakeholders without emotional intelligence, and a problematic team member. My manager and I shared an ambivalence toward one another that deepened during the pandemic. While I was happy and grateful for the opportunities, I was still striving to obtain perfection. My

Chapter 4
Kindness Changes Everything

profession looks easy on the surface, so there are natural critics everywhere, but this was different. Some mornings I would feel like I had been punched in the face even before getting out of bed. I desperately wanted to make things work because I was in love with the work and the opportunities it created. Unconsciously, I returned to a familiar pattern: adopting the behaviors of those around me and of ghosts passed to get ahead. I'd thought that the monster in me was dead and buried, but she was very much alive.

I eventually had to fire my problematic employee—a first in my career. I thought I had made the best choice in a replacement, but job interviews are like speed dating. I quickly learned that their work and communication style were the opposite of mine. My specialty is in communication styles, and I spent years flexing to lawyers, but I couldn't handle this. I was fighting so many battles, exhausted, and still on my perfection mission. I could not adapt to this person and found myself treating them just like my boss in that first law firm had treated me. I knew it was wrong, but I could not help myself. I thought that if I made sure all was perfect, the critics would stop. Looking back, I deeply regret this behavior as a woman and leader.

The events of 2020 brought terror and upheaval. It was also a powerful catalyst for change, whether we wanted it or not. For me, it led to a rapid decline in my mental and physical health. Work became my escape, the only thing I had to look forward to each day, and at the same time, the tension with my boss grew to the point of unbearable. I then lost the "go-to" person on my team to another company. Even as my own misery worsened, however, I realized that everyone was going through something; it was not all about me. I reflected on how my boss was making me feel—and the fact that I too had been way too harsh on my remaining employee. I vowed to destroy the monster and never put perfection above kindness again. I started asking myself if it was even possible to be perfect (and concluded it's not). I had many heart-to-hearts with my employee with the intention to empower and coach, rather than reprimand. While they eventually moved on, I was proud of where that relationship landed—a sentiment they echoed, adding that it was a blessing for something positive to come out of such a terrible time. ***Kindness changed everything.***

Maintaining Me

As the pandemic wore on, so did my need to mix things up. I changed jobs again, surprising myself by returning to the legal industry. This has not been without its challenges, but my transformation allowed me to shift my energy to a more productive space. Each day, I aim to focus on keeping transparency and kindness at the forefront of my interactions. These qualities have improved my ability to be seen as a leader, trusted advisor, and role model, so I have woven them further into my personal management style.

As the world continues to become more uncertain, I don't want to lose myself again in negativity or pressure. We cannot control the personalities, reactions, and situations we encounter. I realize now that I was afraid to show kindness at work because I did not want to be considered timid, weak, or unintelligent. I thought I had to be cruel, uncaring, and at times gossipy to get my seat at the table. While I regret how some of my behaviors impacted people throughout my career, I am grateful for the lessons I learned and my ability to apply them to my leadership skills. I have noticed a collective shift, where it is acceptable and even encouraged to be both emotionally and intellectually intelligent. Each time I feel like I'm getting lost again, I focus on one or more of the following pieces of advice in order to maintain me, no matter the circumstance.

Chapter 4
Kindness Changes Everything

Composure is Crucial. If you are not in the frame of mind to have a conversation about a mistake, challenge, or other difficult situation, do not act immediately. Do not focus on accusations, focus on empowerment. There is no right or wrong way in communication preferences, so understand that your style may be different from the recipient's.

Stand up for YOU. Do not be afraid to speak up when you feel unfairly challenged in a conflict. Stay true to yourself and be professional. I was able to do this more easily after I turned forty, but don't let age hold you back.

Own the Truth. Be direct and forthcoming in your communications. People cannot read your mind, no matter what level you operate at professionally. I often tell people, "I can't fix it if I don't know about it."

Evaluate the Challenge. In a high-pressure world and workplace, people will overreact. Each time I see this happening, I ask myself, "Am I doing brain surgery?" The inevitable answer—NO—reminds me to keep things in perspective and act appropriately. Keeping calm builds credibility.

Boundaries aren't Bad. By not resting, we are being unkind to ourselves, our loved ones, and our places of employment. We cannot be the person we need to be at home and at work without taking proper care of ourselves. The email responses can wait—discern between what is truly urgent and, if it's not, know it's okay to turn off your phone!

I am still a product of my environment and a recovering perfectionist, but I no longer pride myself in how fast I learn and work. Instead, I'm proud of my ability to work hard, be transparent, and actively listen. Recently, I was told by a former employee of my current firm, "Thank you, Sabrina, for having such a calming presence. We need more kind people like you." I was touched knowing that my transformation is completely visible to others. It's true... ***kindness changes everything***.

ABOUT THE AUTHOR: Dr. Sabrina Franconeri is an Amazon International best-selling author, coach, and learning and development professional. Dr. Franconeri has spent more than twenty years teaching the importance of understanding communication styles. Born in Ft. Lauderdale, Florida, she spent much of her life in Pittsburgh, Pennsylvania, earning her Doctor of Science in Communications from Robert Morris University. She has lived in Washinton, D.C. and currently lives and works in the New York City area. Dr. Franconeri loves to travel and considers Hawaii her home away from home. She attributes her love of learning to her parents.

Dr. Sabrina Franconeri
sabrinafranconeri.com
sabrina@sabrinafranconeri.com
412-414-6436

CHAPTER 5

Dragons It Is, Then!
When I Finally Put the Pieces Together, I Knew What the Answer Was

Barbara A. Worsley

Merlin had been in my life long before I recognized him. I remember when that happened. It was a cold, crisp fall day in the northeastern USA, and I had just stepped out of a twenty-four-year marriage. I was walking my dog, as I did every day, but for some reason I was struck by how vibrant the colors of the foliage were!

How had I not seen this before?

Ah! I thought to myself, *I am seeing life differently.* Then I heard a voice that sounded reassuring.

"YES, Dear One, you are seeing life with new eyes."

I looked around and caught sight of him out of the corner of my eye—a wizard, standing by the tree. He was just how I had imagined Merlin, with long gray hair and beard; a pointed hat with stars on it; long, flowing blue robe, and a very large staff with delicate carvings.

"Hello. I am Merlin."

This was the first of many conversations I would have with Merlin in those early days of seeing and hearing life differently. It was like someone had turned on the lights.

Over the next few years, I discovered Reiki, Polarity therapy, and The Universal Kabbalah, and many other modalities that I would integrate into my work as a hands-on healer.

Reiki is an ancient Japanese form of energy healing using the hands through which universal energy flows—the hands placed on a person can increase the flow of energy to help healing. The underlying concept of Polarity therapy is that all energy within the body is based on electromagnetic forces. Disease results from improperly dissipated energy; however, by placing hands on the person different energy pathways can be unblocked and restored. Universal Kabbalah is the study of The Tree of Life, and answers the questions: Who am I? What am I? Where did I come from? What is my purpose?

This was also when I encountered angels, archangels, and higher dimensions, though I would not know for many years how important this study would be for me. Angels are spiritual beings who serve God and humanity. Archangels are past spiritual masters who have walked this Earth and are tasked with managing life here, including creation, soul contracts, and the spiritual development of all souls. Each archangel has a different area of expertise.

I continued to have conversations with Merlin and other ascended masters, angels, and archangels—often communicating through automatic writing. Also called psychography, this is the psychic ability to produce written words without consciously writing them—rather like a surprise at the end of a poem!

Though I loved exploring these gifts, my physical reality—that of a single parent to two teenage boys—was demanding my full attention. I found myself working two jobs to bring in enough money to keep a roof over our heads and food on the table.

Chapter 5
Dragons It Is, Then!

The Next Big Steps

Over the years, things began to ease up, and eventually I got a new job that allowed me to work Monday through Friday. However, it wasn't until 2021 that I experienced a dramatic shift. I decided I would "take the year" to discover and renew the gifts or modalities suited to me. If anyone had told me what the outcome of this spiritual quest would be I would not have believed them. I do remember saying, "Just show me. What am I supposed to do?" and finding online a spiritual community based in Arizona.

It brought me to a place where I felt safe and was able to pick up where I'd left off years ago. Soon I was back to my automatic writing, learning and brushing up on my spiritual knowledge; I was also taking classes and learning about new approaches to ancient wisdoms—including an in-person, four-day Mind, Body, Spirit Practitioners class.

As I was preparing for my trip, I felt like something big was about to happen, and it was going to happen fast. It certainly began with a whirlwind—an Uber from the airport to the hotel for my first night, then a second ride to the Airbnb I was renting with four women I had not even met. I had arrived in the land of being guided and trusting the process!

A few weeks later, during a meeting with my spiritual community, I asked for a message from Spirit, as I felt that others were getting answers to their questions while mine had gone unaddressed.

"At the end, you will receive a message," I heard.

Sure enough, as we were about to wrap up, the group's facilitator suddenly asked me, "Why are you not using your gift?" She then turned to the group and said, "Barbara channels Ascended Masters."

WOW…I channel!! For those who don't know, channeling is a "new age" word for a person who serves as a medium for Spirit

(i.e., "She channels Elvis.")

The minute I said, "I am a channel," *and* embraced it, life changed. And, as I continued to claim that gift, I was increasingly awestruck by my connections and the clarity that came with them.

I settled in for the ride, connecting with Ascended Masters like Mother Mary, Mary Magdalen, St Germain, Isis, Kuan Yin, Cleopatra, Mother Gaia, Merlin and his wife, and The Christ consciousness. I was also remembering my past life connections in Atlantis and Lemuria.

I kept asking, *What does all of this mean? Where is this taking me?*

No answer came, so I kept writing and asking. Then, during a session of writing, I got the name Commander Ashtar from Galactic Command.

Galactic Command? I just had to google that!

I learned that, yes, there was a Galactic Commander Ashtar—a name given to an extraterrestrial being or group of beings first channeled in 1952. Ashtar command is a galactic law enforcement agency preparing to rescue humanity. It was also to be my connection to many more ETs over the coming months. Currently, I am talking with beings from other worlds and planets.

When I get a feeling, or "nudge," like someone wants to speak with me, I sit down and allow the messages to flow, and at the end I am told who the person/being/name is. Everyone channels differently, but I have recognized that it comes more easily for me than for some others. I learned why during one of many conversations with my guides.

My daily practice of grounding myself firmly in Mother Gaia each day has allowed me to reach higher dimensional beings.

"The deeper you ground yourself," I was told, "the higher

Chapter 5
Dragons It Is, Then!

vibrations you can access."

Grounding is connecting with earth's surface by direct or intended contact with the Earth. I like to visualize roots growing from the bottom of my feet and going deep down into Mother Gaia, wrapping them around a rock to firmly hold me in Her energy. I also imagine a root growing from the base of my spine, and going deep down into the Earth and wrapping that around a rock. Then, I am firmly grounded and can connect with my day, my spirit, or both.

I noticed that I often received messages during my daily walks, and on one sunny day in the summer of 2022, I heard "look up."

I looked up, and there, right above me, were dragons flying and frolicking in the blue skies amidst the clouds. Thinking this cannot really be happening, I pulled out my phone and began snapping pictures. DRAGONS! They were telling me they were my sky dragons. When I got home, I looked at the ten or so photos and, yes—they were dragons, six *very* large dragons.

OMG! Now what…?

Things were quiet for a few days—I posted my pictures on Facebook and got a few likes, though no comments that I remember. Then, after I had time to think on the encounter, messages came in fast. Again, these were not just from the dragons, but from Ascended Masters working with dragons, so it was no big surprise when Merlin's dragon made himself known to me, as did Lord Kuthami—a dragon elder.

I started to look for dragons and looked for information to understand why they were showing up for me. According to what I read, dragons were appearing to more and more people as Earth wakes up to their presence. Dragons have been around Earth since "the dawn of time." They work with many Ascended Masters and Archangels and Galactics. I soon found out that my dragons were, in fact, Galactic dragons, and I was being asked to work directly with the Galactic Realm.

Now I want to share with you some of the channeled messages I've received (through automatic writing)—the first from Merlin's wife.

"Speak from your heart—all the ways you can.

You cannot ever doubt the true message when it is heart-centered.

Breathe from your heart space.

Love from your heart.

See only from your heart's eyes.

Do not listen to those who say, "Use your head not your heart."

I am Gwendolyn—I walk with you each day.

Holding your hand.

Merlin is your teacher—I am your heart.

Much love and gratitude,

Gwendolyn

The following is from Commander Ashtar:

Star command tuning into your request

Sending you visual downloads

Sacred geometry is a communication tool too

Thank you, Dear One, for tuning into my energy.

Indeed, the visuals you are receiving are also memories, I see past memories slipping into your conscious mind.

It all means something on your life journey on Earth.

All you are & have been working on:

Karma

Clearing pathways

Clearing and opening your heart space

Connect telepathically to us & Ascended Masters

Chapter 5
Dragons It Is, Then!

Connecting with Mother Gaia
Connecting with our Star fleet
Seeing and hearing about the brothers and sisters in light.
Memories
Dreams
All of these are memories of what has been, where you have been, and where you will return.
We hold that for you
Just know that you are multidimensional
No secret
We all are...
Your message from us today, and of course Ashtar is...
Continue walking your current path
Keep your head held high
Tap into our knowledge
Tap into our being.
We are protecting you
Guiding you
So many masters are appearing to you, so you can feel the love and respect for every light being.
There are NO BARRIERS here above the 5th dimension.
No better, no worse.
No good or bad.
We just are who we are.
So refreshing for you Earthbound beings right now.
War and unrest are holding your earth hostage at this time.
We are sad to see such rebellion.
We are sad that the human race is so angry. STILL.
We hold Earth in our hands and send what we can to those with open hearts.
Those who are called to hear these messages realize that Mother Earth sheds tears as She feels the anger rage in her

belly.

Like all mothers, she wants Peace & Calm but can only watch as Earth continues to be angry and hurting.

Light workers send your precious earth

LOVE, LIGHT & HEALING

Every drop ripples across continents and countries.

PRAY for your brothers and sisters in light—PRAY.

There is so much love for you all to receive, open your arms, receive our love and light and in return send this back to us.

Be still in your day to listen to the downloads we are sending to you.

It may be shapes

It may be words

Or just reminders and Memories

Cherish them all.

With love in our hearts for all of you,

Ashtar & the Star Command

My name, EAST COAST DRAGON LADY, was acquired "by accident." I was channeling dragons, reading dragon cards when I was in a Facebook group meeting when the host asked which Barbara is this?

"Why," I quipped, "I'm The East Coast Dragon Lady."

Everyone loved it!

Since I have accepted and embraced that I am a channel and healer, life is moving at a fast pace. New experiences are happening on a daily basis. I am connecting to high vibrational beings of love and light. I am remembering my past (lives) and what my final destination in this incarnation will be.

I have always believed I will move on from this Earthly plane when I finally cross the Rainbow Bridge—to carry on what I started many, many moons ago. In the meantime, I share the messages I

Chapter 5
Dragons It Is, Then!

receive and the modalities I've learned to help heal the world.

ABOUT THE AUTHOR: Born in London, Barbara spent many years working as a registered nurse (RN) before moving to the USA in the early 1990s. She is much better known, however, as the East Coast Dragon Lady & Galactic Dragon Ambassador, the channel to many ascended masters, galactics, and dragons. She has studied many modalities over the years and is a Mind Body Spirit practitioner using reiki & polarity in combination as a hands-on healer. Barbara is the mother of two adult sons and lives in Amesbury, Massachusetts.

Barbara A. Worsley
eastcoastdragonlady@gmail.com
eastcoastdragonlady.com

CHAPTER 6

If My Body Quits, Where Am I Going to Live?

Suzy Rawlins

In October 2022, I planned a girls' weekend in Sedona with my cousin "Toots" and my BFF from childhood. At the last minute, my friend got sick and had to stay home, but since the trip was already paid for, Toots and I went anyway. Though we missed her, it was such a peaceful, relaxing, and reinvigorating weekend, and, for me, just what the doctor ordered. For the past few months, I had felt stuck. I was going through the motions but did not see the results. That is because, though I didn't realize it, my heart was not really invested. Shortly after that trip, I had an ah-ha moment, and that's when my latest journey began.

But before we go into that, let me share the backstory. Travel back with me about seventeen years ago, 2005, when I first heard the word cancer. In truth, it was pre-cancer, but still scary as hell. I was a single mama working several jobs to make a life for my boys. I went through a simple procedure that should have taken care of it. At this point, I told no one except one very close friend. In 2007, I enrolled in school to become a licensed massage therapist.

Only three months into the one-year program, I became very ill. After several medical tests to find the problem, it was determined that the cancer had returned to my cervix and that my thyroid was completely out of control. I graduated from massage school in October 2008 and had a total thyroidectomy two weeks later. A post-surgery biopsy confirmed that I'd had a malignant tumor on my thyroid, and it was an excellent decision to take it out. I then received some radiation to ensure the cancer was gone; just one month later, I had another surgery to eliminate the cancer on my cervix. I have been fortunate never to have chemo, only surgeries and small amounts of radiation. Due to these new health scares, I postponed getting my massage license to focus on my health. If I am being honest, I feel that God led me to this school so I could learn so much more about human anatomy and pathology.

In 2009, I remarried an incredible man and amazing stepdad to my boys. I also started a business. Opportunity had knocked a few times before, but the time was right for me to hear the opportunity and embrace it. At this point, I took the leap of faith to join a direct sales company, even though I had no clue how to use their products. I was willing to learn, though, and after a lot of networking in my area, I built a large clientele.

Shortly after that, I fought a horrible staph infection. It took seven rounds of antibiotics to knock it out, finally. Well, by that point, my immune system had tanked. My doctor recommended I get the flu shot to be safe since my immune system was not good. I had never taken it before but thought it was better to be safe than sorry. That led to seven months of pneumonia and bronchitis back-to-back. Never again, I said, no more flu shots for me, and my doctor agreed. I thought there had to be a better way. So, I started researching

Chapter 6
If My Body Quits, Where Am I Going to Live?

natural remedies. With no formal education, I did a fantastic job keeping myself healthy for many years. I had no choice either; I had no health insurance.

All through 2011 and 2012, I had been having lower right-side pain. I knew it was my ovaries, but what do I know? I am not a doctor; I am, after all, the one living in this body. They found nothing through all kinds of scans, ultrasounds, and tests. Well, not nothing, but nothing Western medicine was willing to help me with. I had several ovarian cysts that kept rupturing and making me violently ill. I also had a period that lasted fifty-nine days and was told that was nothing to worry about. In late 2012, they finally did exploratory surgery (they said it was my last option to find out why I had the pain). This surgery resulted in the most incredible images of my ovaries, showing why they needed to be removed. The surgeon took my appendix then because he said it was unhealthy and would eventually burst. I trusted this surgeon with my life; he was the one who did my thyroidectomy. So, when it came time for exploratory, I asked if I could choose him again. I took the ovary images to my OBGYN, and she suggested I have only the right one removed. I was tired of surgery and all the recovery; honestly, I felt like a "pick-a-part" at this point, so I requested a total hysterectomy.

In 2014, we had a house fire and lost everything. We are grateful to the community and networking friends for all the incredible donations to help us rebuild our lives. That year held much tragedy for us as well. That fall, we made a sudden decision to homeschool our boys. I swore I would never be a teacher, and now here I was, homeschooling my kids with the help of my mom, a retired teacher. We got our boys involved in 4H, showing hogs—something I always wanted to do as a kid but never had the opportunity to do. Who knew it was a beauty pageant for hogs? I definitely did not, but it was a fun and educational experience!

In 2016, we had the opportunity to take care of my eighty-nine-year-old Great Uncle Buck for the last eight months of this life. He was mostly independent at that point and came to live with us just for extra eyes and help; however, fifteen days later, he fell and broke his humerus. From that point on, he was full lift and assist. I swore I would never be a nurse, yet here I was, caring for my uncle. Honestly, I had to do a lot of research about how to use a gate belt and other things to help him. Uncle Buck was wheelchair-bound; however, we took him on many field trips with the homeschool and even took him to the county fair, where our boys showed hogs. We did not allow him being in a wheelchair to stop us from giving him the best experiences for the last part of his life.

Also, in 2016, the home we had been renting was going up for sale, so we had to move. All the animals and Uncle Buck had to go with us. I lived in the far west valley almost all my life, so we had been looking only at that part of town. Well, God found us a home near the city of Maricopa, the opposite side of town, and a different county—meaning I had to build a new customer base. I put myself out there—networking, joining the chamber of commerce, and showing up everywhere. I built a new network and clientele in my new city and surrounding area.

In 2016, I started having leg pain, not knowing what it was. Electrolytes seemed to help. I also had what we thought were kidney stones. I went to the ER after passing out from pain (I had given birth twice with no medication and did not feel it; my pain threshold is super high). They dismissed me, just saying I had a UTI. Seriously, I'm not a fan of Western medicine.

Chapter 6
If My Body Quits, Where Am I Going to Live?

In 2019, my real healing journey began. I always wanted to see a naturopathic doctor; they were all in the East Valley when I was in the West Valley. In my heart, I felt that I also wanted a traditional healer as my doctor. Well, now I know why God brought us to Maricopa. That is where I met Dr. Yolanda Rodriguez, ND, and WOW, she helped change my life. I am eternally grateful for her healing and our friendship. She has taught me not to mask the symptoms but to genuinely heal my body. I started seeing Dr. Yolanda in about 2018 for my thyroid medication maintenance and checking my hormones and blood work. In 2019, I thought I was having a heart attack at a steakhouse while out with my family. I'd had enough human anatomy education to know that it was not my heart, but my digestive system. I put it off a week or so before going to the ER. They treated me like crap but ran tests and labs, which I immediately took to Dr Yolanda. She would heal me and not just treat the symptoms. So, it was August 2019 when she ran a food sensitivity panel on me. OH, MY GOODNESS…My list was long.

What was I willing to do to get my health back? Everything necessary. It started with a ninety-day detox (from September through November), and I did great through the holidays. During this time, I also was using a rebounder to get my lymphatic fluid moving, as well as leg compression socks, a compression massager, and a lot of dry brushing. I won't lie: I got lazy in 2020 with my food restrictions. I turned forty in July of that year and needed to get back on track. The serious inflammation and lymphatic fluid that my body was holding was painful. So, under the supervision of Dr. Yolanda, I did a seven-day fasting/detox. Then I rolled right into a ninety-day candida-free diet (again, hard, but worth it), then completed another seven-day fasting/detox. Now that I felt like my gut was healing and I felt better every day, it was time to get more active.

Since the world was shut down, I started hiking with a friend in October 2020. We found a fun challenge to hike one hundred miles in a hundred days, and the prize was a t-shirt. Hey, whatever gets you moving, right? I chose to do another fasting/detox after we completed that challenge. I learned that periods of fasting made my body feel good. We continued to hike through May that year. It is now a thing, hiking from fall through spring for mental health and fitness. I was super excited when I completed my first 5K on May 5, 2021, another 5K on Memorial Day and a third in June. Now that my health was better and I was getting more physically fit, it was time to get mentally fit. I decided to start the 75 Hard Challenge on May 18 and successfully completed it in one attempt. It was one of the most challenging things I ever did. Getting up every day and completing the grueling tasks. I fought through two horrible UTIs and a foot injury but was determined to finish. I even remember jumping out of bed to take the darn picture; I was not failing the challenge because I was not taking a picture. I even had to work out in the dark and rain a few times. It was not pretty, but it was done, and I am proud of myself.

I share all the grueling and challenging things I did to take my health back because I want you to know that although it was not easy, it was worth it. I did everything, and I mean EVERYTHING, my ND suggested, even if it did not make sense at the time. The results showed up and proved to me that I was on the right track.

Through my gut healing journey, I have encouraged my sister and her family to get food sensitivity tested. My youngest son and Toots have also done the test and are now learning to eat to nourish

Chapter 6
If My Body Quits, Where Am I Going to Live?

their bodies.

Welcome back to October 2022. Let me introduce you to the woman I am today. I am a confident, genuinely healthy, back-to-my-roots farmgirl who is spiritually grounded, proud of my two adult boys, and a happy wife for more than fourteen years to my wonderful hubby, Guy. I have been blessed to attend many retreats and conferences led by incredible leaders and mentors. I read daily to grow and learn. I am back to being physically active like I was many years ago. I am very intentional about my health and my body. Over the past three years, with the help of my excellent naturopathic doctor, I have been able to heal my gut and dramatically improve my overall health.

Now, it is time to get back to that ah-ha moment I mentioned in the beginning. I realized that my true gift was to help others live intentionally. Through reflection, I decided to enroll in school to become a Holistic Health and Wellness Coach with a focus on nutrition. I am about halfway through the program and feel this is where I am called to and want to serve. I want to serve at a deeper level. The world would be better if more people knew that there were more natural remedies and that self-care and personal growth make a HUGE difference in their lives. I am only one voice; however, I can use that voice to share my knowledge and experience. Everything I do today, tomorrow, and the next day is to leave a legacy. Someone is waiting for me to learn more and share more.

I am finally following the path God has cleared and prepared me for over the last two decades. I am pursuing my passion for helping others live intentionally. My journey led me to know in my heart and soul how important it is for me to help others get spiritually grounded, find nutrition that heals their body, develop unbridled confidence, and genuinely fall in love with their whole life.

ABOUT THE AUTHOR: Suzy Rawlins is a holistic health and wellness coach and a farmgirl at heart whose mission is to continually change and improve her life and the lives of others. She has visited and talked with hundreds of people throughout her various careers, and these conversations all brought her back to the same point: Live Intentionally. She has combined her passion for service, formal training and education, and knowledge from her own healing journey to help people live their best lives. She shares with them her process for intentional living, working with them to set goals, develop a plan, and take inspired action.

Suzy Rawlins
Roots & Boots Intentional Living
suzyrawlins.com
suzy@suzyrawlins.com
623-451-7780

CHAPTER 7

Life is Full of Adventure
If You are Willing to Accept It
Diana Cockle

My belief that life is an adventure probably stems from where I grew up—Powell, Wyoming. If you are not familiar with that, perhaps you have heard of Yellowstone National Park? Yep, that was our backyard, and we loved all of it. We took many family trips to Yellowstone. Sometimes, we would go with my dad alone on his motorcycle. I have countless memories—from camping or making a fire, to having a little lunch by the river, to seeing Old Faithful and observing the thousands of wildlife species that call it home.

My work adventure started when I was fourteen, as a home caregiver for a next-door neighbor who needed a little TLC. My mother was a nurse and I often thought I would follow in her footsteps; however, I also recall wanting from a young age to be a hairdresser. The idea of talking to and working on people was exciting to me. I gave my first "haircut"—to myself—at age five. And, wouldn't you know, it was the day before picture day. I was so proud of myself as I showed off my new bangs. Mom had me dressed in a very bright red and yellow dress, and there across my forehead was what appeared to be a jack-o-lantern smile (aka, my bangs). She hid the scissors after that, but I still found them from time to time. All of my Barbies got haircuts, though oddly enough, I never wanted to cut my brother or sister's hair—probably a good thing!

    I wasted no time in pursuing my dream. After graduating from Central High School in Grand Forks, North Dakota, I began the cosmetology course at the Hair Designers Academy. I was thrilled as we had to wear uniforms and the attire was strict in how it was worn and laundered. My first time taking a client, I was so nervous I spent more time in the bathroom throwing up than I did behind the chair! Thankfully, one of my wonderful instructors helped to ease me through that first cut. I felt sorry for the client, though, of course, they had to be pretty brave to sit in that chair in the first place.

    I remember a visit from my parents after I graduated and had a cosmetology job. Dad never let me cut his hair; he was very old school and went to a barber. Mom was a different story. She had the most beautiful hair with natural curls; she was also adventurous enough to get in my chair. That was the first of many haircuts I would give her. I always did something different, and her nursing colleagues would ooooohhh and aaaaahhh over what she had done. It's hard to believe that I have been a cosmetologist for thirty-six years now, though these days the only time I'm "behind the chair" is to make sure my husband looks sharp.

    It wasn't long, maybe two years, before I started to think, "Is this all I am going to do with my life?" There was a downtime in between customers at the salon, which resulted in lots of conversations about what folks were doing in their various careers. Computers were starting to become all the rage and I was quick at learning. So off I went, seeking something I could do in an office setting. My first office job was with RGIS Inventory Services, and it was an

Chapter 7
Life is Full of Adventure

experience that really opened my eyes. I learned a lot about retail, store set-ups, and the value of what is in those brick-and-mortar stores. For a while I worked for RGIS part-time in addition to cutting hair, and I even had a side hustle cleaning houses. Are you getting the vibe that I love to keep busy?

I was brought up with a strong work ethic—and the belief that one should stay with one company and give it one hundred percent each and every day. My mother worked for the same hospital for twenty-five years. My dad farmed for twenty-five-plus years and then drove a bus and was the groundskeeper for our community college for more than ten. My grandfather worked for the railroad for thirty-five years. Yet, I found staying in the same job so boring and was always searching for something new, something challenging, something fun, something rewarding and fulfilling. I enjoyed updating my resume, going to interviews, learning about different companies, and acquiring new skills. I have worked for some well-known financial corporations, a fire protection agency as a design administrative assistant, along with compliance and procedures companies.

Without a doubt, one of my wildest jobs was for EMSI, a drug collection agency. Businesses contracted us to do random drug testing, as well as screenings for new hires, life insurance policies, and genetic testing. The completion of these drug screenings sometimes resulted in additional contact with our office. A person would say one thing, and next thing you know, you were getting a phone call from a spouse or Mother begging to not send in the test due to positive drugs in the person's system. Oftentimes, I knew they were lying anyway—by that time, I had worked in hair for many years and my people skills were sharp. Here's a hint, folks: tell the truth the first time.

I even went to the Scottsdale Culinary Institute and became a pastry chef! Now, I no longer create lavish desserts like I did while I was there, but I can easily whip up four to six dozen cookies in no time. Culinary school also turned me into a food snob. While my husband will always choose In-n-Out Burger, I prefer the fare of gourmet chefs. My all-time favorite is Gordon Ramsey, and we never fail to dine at one of his restaurants when we go to Las Vegas.

During my forty-one years of working, I have met some of the most amazing people, many of whom are still part of my life today. I have also lived in six different states. I had never even visited Arizona when I learned the financial institution I was working for had an opening there and in one of the departments I'd had my eye on for years. I jumped at the opportunity and moved to Arizona in just two weeks, never looking back. I met my wonderful husband, Peter, here in Arizona. (We lived on opposite ends of the golf course.) He is my partner in crime, my motivator and cheerleader, my companion, my everything. I owe my adventures to him. As he will say, "Go for it." He completes me.

It was not an easy decision to leave my corporate job to work with Peter in his logistics business—an industry he has been in for thirty-six years. Most married couples could never do this, but we love it and would not have it any other way. My husband, who originally hails from England, is also an all-around soccer guru with various certifications and trainings in the sport. A year or so ago he was doing things that would change how we worked our logistics business. With this soccer adventure, it would involve things traveling globally. While this was going on, I had to stop and think about what I was going to do, I am not one to just sit and do nothing. I started thinking about when and where we may go, what I could do while he was out doing his thing and in any city or country. What about flowers? I could visit flower shops in different

Chapter 7
Life is Full of Adventure

cities and countries and continue to learn new things. Possibly get hands-on with some popular flower shops or hotels.

Michael Gaffney of American School of Flower Design has sixteen schools around the globe, and when my friend Janeen Sanderson told me she had completed a class at his Phoenix location, I thought it sounded like so much fun! I signed up for a week-long training with Michael and was hooked from the first day. I had no idea where this beautiful world of flowers would lead me, but I knew life would never be the same.

It has also connected me with some very dear friends in our community. Being able to create arrangements for their lives is beyond fulfilling. As of May 29, 2023, I have been a florist for 1 year, I have launched my business, Royal Blooms, LLC, had a website created, www.royalbloomsllc.com, and have competed in floral competitions. In addition, I took several on-hand education courses and became a Master Florist in the State of Arizona—all while still working side by side with my amazing husband, who supports me in all that I do.

Most people tend to stay in the same job for years, just going through the motions and looking forward to retirement. I honestly do not know if that will ever happen. I love a challenge and an adventure. I can work with flowers anywhere on this earth. With flowers, one will never stop learning. Keeping up with trends, colors, arranging, and designing makes my heart full; it's my passion. Think about when you received flowers; how did it make you feel? Flowers are for any occasion; in times of death, they can aide in remembering that loved one, and they can rejoice the person who is dealing with the loss of their loved ones. Flowers bring comfort and joy to those who are sick, need a pick me up, just because, or for a spouse that is sorry for the fight they have had. Men, if you have a fight with your spouse, pick an arrangement or a large number of roses depending on how mad she is. It will be worth it; I can promise you that!

How did this little girl from Wyoming manage to do all of these things in her fifty-five years on this earth? I had the most amazing mother and her wisdom stays with me today. I also ensure that I surround myself with positive people who build me up as I do them. As I mentioned previously, my husband, with all his love and support, helps me to get up each morning and do it all over again and again. I must mention my love of dogs too. My two boys are my world, and being able to be with them 24/7 as they get on in years is heartwarming for me.

I can remember from a very young age my mother telling me to always smile and make eye contact with people. She said, "You never know what they are going through or if they may be alone and perhaps do not have family." To this day, I find it is heart-filling when you get smiles back and more so when people stop and talk to you. We need more of this in our world. I challenge people to compliment someone that you do not know when you are out and about. Watch how people react. Watch their facial expressions. Check out how their posture changes or a little extra hop in their step.

I have been beyond blessed to be on this earth and experience so many wonderful things and not-so-wonderful things. Those not-wonderful things have given me strength to do more. To take risks and challenges. To find out who I am and to become this amazing woman with a hidden talent in flowers. I do not know what the future holds for me in flowers. What I can tell you is that I love them and creating arrangements for people. I can imagine a piece in my head that will get created by touching my heart and radiate to my hands to create something that is already beautiful into something beyond

Chapter 7
Life is Full of Adventure

amazing. I do feel flowers are my passion, just like the passion I have for my fabulous husband.

Just remember, you are never too old to learn something new and to take those opportunities, so jump in and enjoy the ride!

ABOUT THE AUTHOR: Diana Cockle is a wife, furmom, entrepreneur, and Master Floral Designer. Over the years she has had the opportunity to live in different places and meet many wonderful people. Now she lives in the city of Maricopa, Arizona with her husband Peter, Scooter, a fourteen-year-old Welsh Pembroke Corgi, and Stallone, a ten-year-old Belgian Malinois. Diana and Peter work together in their logistics business, shipping LTL shipments all over the world. She also has a passion for flowers and plants, and recently launched a floral business, then returned to school to get her Master Floral Degree.

Diana Cockle
Royal Blooms LLC
facebook.com/groups/maricoparoyalblooms
royalbloomsllc@gmail.com
520-252-1301

CHAPTER 8

From Fired to Fantastic

Wil Becker

Back in 2014, I found myself in a challenging situation at work. My team lead, Don, was trying to get me fired, and though I wasn't entirely sure why, I suspected it stemmed from conversations we had as we got to know each other. I must have said things that offended him, because it was clear that he didn't like me. The stress and fear of working under him was also bleeding into my home life—often in the form of nightmares that he would show up at my home one morning before work and fire me. I still can see him in my mind's eye, parking his gold sedan in the visitor parking in front of my townhouse, walking up to my door, and knocking on it to tell me I no longer had a job.

One day in April, Don called me into a meeting with the program manager (PM) and the deputy program manager (DPM). To my dismay, I was presented with a write-up, also known as a "Ninety-day Personal Improvement Plan" (PIP). There were five issues in my PIP, none of which I had been aware of before that meeting. I knew Don's intention was to get me fired that day…but it didn't work. After enduring fifteen minutes of getting yelled at and saying "Yes, sir" a lot, I walked out with a signed copy of my write-up.

After the meeting, the DPM asked to speak with me privately.

As we walked back toward my desk, he informed me that he would be going on our next scheduled business trip. While we were there, he said, he would like to speak to me about what had happened.

I wasn't sure what to expect when, a few weeks later, the DPM and I met in a private room at his hotel. He first informed me that what Don had done was wrong and not the way our company did things. He also let me know that Don was reprimanded for the PIP. Then, over the next forty-five minutes, he listened to my side of the story and mentored me on what to do next. First, I was to turn around and face Don whenever he came to speak to me. Second, I was to call Don "sir" and be very respectful in the way I spoke to him. I didn't feel that I had been disrespectful of Don, but I was willing to do anything I could to change the atmosphere in the office—and keep my job.

After that trip, I followed the DPM's advice diligently. Slowly, over the rest of that year, things improved. At the end of 2014, however, I was put on another PIP because I had argued with Don. I had just finished working directly with our project manager when Don asked me to secure a container. I didn't understand why he was telling me to do this, as I had finished that task with the PM. Finally, after several minutes of yelling at me, he told me to do it because the PM had called him and asked that I double-check our work. I was feeling very frustrated by this because knowing all of the details would have changed the way I had received the instructions in the first place. I was struggling with Don's leadership style and desire for his team to follow instructions blindly.

In September 2015, my life took another difficult turn when my family lost our home to foreclosure. Determined to fix our financial situation, I embarked on a journey of self-improvement. After a few years of listening to audios, reading books, watching videos, and

Chapter 8
From Fired to Fantastic

following several online personalities, I had learned a good bit of information, yet I was still struggling to implement that information.

During this time, my relationship with Don had continued to improve. Then, while on a business trip in 2017, I got shocking news from him. On two occasions, he had completely lost balance and fell—once hitting his head seriously enough that his son insisted he get it checked out. After the appointment, Don called to inform me that I would be running our team for a few months. He had a malignant tumor the size of a baseball in his brain, and he was headed to surgery that Saturday!

Don gave me all the instructions I needed to pick up his workload. I was sent a few resumes to conduct interviews for him and make hiring decisions for our team. I had meetings to attend and other responsibilities that he asked me to pick up while he was in recovery, while still maintaining my usual workload. It was a huge surprise that he was willing to ask me to step up and for him to hand off the team lead responsibilities to me. Over the next three months, I filled in while he went through recovery and physical therapy.

It soon became apparent that Don would not return to work. At this point, we also had a new PM who recommended me to take the team lead position; however, the contract director didn't think that I was a good fit. The PM and DPM fought for me, but it fell on deaf ears. A woman named Lisa was hired as the team lead while I continued to run the daily operations.

In early 2018, I was introduced to a learning platform and leadership organization. It is a supportive community with information that—thanks to my three years of research and learning—I recognized as world-class. I joined the organization, and as I learned from the leaders, audios, and recommended books, I started to notice some amazing changes.

The constant travel and ongoing stress had a huge impact on my home life. I felt disconnected from my wife and kids because no one wanted to be around me and my short temper. I struggled to relax or play with my kids because my thoughts always came back to the situation at work.

It was while on a business trip that I recognized the transformation that was taking place. One evening, my wife called to check in on me. After the typical greeting and my update on the flight, she told me that my three youngest boys had cried themselves to sleep that night because I wasn't there to tuck them into bed. This shocked me because I had gone on many such trips, and they had never seemed to miss me before! Three weeks later, after returning home from yet another trip, I received more proof that I had changed: those boys climbed on my lap as we watched a movie together after dinner.

I was learning to better manage my emotions and handle work at work, then leave it there when I headed home. I was figuring out how to release the stress and find joy in the journey of discovery and growth! I was able to find ways to relieve my overall anxiety about life in general. Listening to audios and reading books inspired me to figure out the things that hurt my mental and emotional health and then work to strengthen those areas. They also helped me to find victories in daily life that helped keep my focus on my goals.

I was no longer the grumpy or angry dad that everyone wanted to avoid. I was becoming more fun and relaxed. I was learning how to respond to each of my kids' needs and personalities, and to communicate better with them and other people. The leadership system gave me tools and examples of how to handle stressful situations and people in mindful and wise ways. This caused me to become more committed to the leadership learning system and to listen to and read even more of the recommended audios and

Chapter 8
From Fired to Fantastic

books. I couldn't believe how much I had changed in just a few months, and I found myself wanting to work with others to help them do the same.

At work, I helped bring Lisa up to speed with our team's work and deliverables. She recognized that I had many skills and attributes outside my job description that would be a benefit to the company. What she saw in me was there because of my personal and professional growth. She started giving me reviews that asked the company to look for and place me in a different position—one that would take advantage of my new leadership and people skills. She wrote things like, "Wil has exceeded all abilities required for this team and would best serve the company, as well as himself, with a more challenging role." She also sent a memo to me in which she expressed her belief that I was capable of so much more than my current position. She wrote that I "continued to exceed expectations on this team" and "was always willing to go the extra mile and help others, without complaining." She even called me "the go-to guy" on the team and spoke of my integrity!

Thanks to the leadership platform, my personal growth and development continued to accelerate! I learned valuable skills like public speaking, personal communication, leadership, and emotional intelligence. I continued to gain insights from the successful individuals speaking on the audios, writing the books, and mentoring sessions I was in. With this newfound confidence, I began to be a leader in my own life and started serving my community and church in better and more specific ways.

As I shared my experiences and wisdom with others, I realized the joy of guiding people on their own personal journey of transformation. Today, I run a growing coaching business. It brings me immense joy to help others change and grow in their personal and professional abilities.

Reading, listening, and associating with positive influences have been crucial in my journey, and I'm passionate about sharing these tools with others and guiding them on their own path to their success. It started with talking to a friend, and from that conversation it gave him the confidence to go after another job, and it increased his income by thirty percent! Then, a friend reached out to tell me he had seen one of my book review videos, and it inspired him to read the book himself. That led him to another leadership book and then to embarking on a physical and mental fitness program.

It is so amazing to watch another person grow. To see them "get" a concept or idea and then implement that into their life! The Facebook Lives, YouTube channel, *Iron Wil's Book Review* podcast, and the quotes I share across social media are all part of my effort to empower and inspire others to lead more fulfilling lives. It is so fascinating to watch, knowing that their journeys will be different from mine but that we are all moving toward our best selves.

In conclusion, my experiences have taught me the importance of personal growth and the impact of good mentors and a supportive community. I'm very excited to continue my own journey and inspire, guide, and mentor others on their own path to personal transformation. This path leads to peace and fulfillment, even while facing—and triumphing over—life's challenges.

ABOUT THE AUTHOR: Wil is a writer, podcaster, speaker, coach, and entrepreneur. He has served in several leadership roles over the last twenty-five years, including Youth Pastor, Congregational Leader, and Assistant Pastor. He has also served with the Boy & Cub Scouts organizations as a Scout Master, Assistant Scout Master, and Den Leader. Wil moved up in his professional career because of his love of technology, leadership skills, and his consistent self-

Chapter 8
From Fired to Fantastic

education. He loves to teach and help others grow and excel, while continuing to learn from the best books, audios, events, and mentors.

Iron Wil Becker
Turning Leaf Solutions
turningleafs.com
wil@turningleafs.com
443-404-7142

CHAPTER 9

Becoming Unshakeable
My Journey from Grief to Empowerment
Margaret Dennis

Have you ever wanted something SO badly that you could taste it?

I have.

I wanted to be a mom.

When I was a little girl, all blonde pigtails, big blue eyes, and dreams of what being a mom would be like, I played with my dolls for hours on end. Rocking them. Feeding them. Changing their diapers. Cuddling them. I could imagine myself as a mom so clearly, holding my baby close to me and pouring all my love into my child. It was the BEST feeling in the world.

Funny how life never quite goes the way you wish it would.

In 2003, we started trying for a family. I was devastated when, after one month, we weren't pregnant. Crazy, I know, but I had BIG expectations and I was SO ready to be a mom—like, NOW! After another three or four months of trying, I still wasn't pregnant. Adding insult to injury was that everywhere I looked, I would see a pregnant woman. It was heartbreaking. Deep down, I knew something was wrong. My intuition knew long before the doctors told us almost a year later.

We had "unexplained" infertility—which basically meant they had absolutely no idea what the problem was.

For the next four years, I was poked and prodded by so many doctors I lost count. I had bloodwork done regularly to check my hormone levels and was given needles to influence my cycle (and I HATE needles!). I lost all sense of dignity, and our privacy was non-existent. Sex was no longer spontaneous and fun and a way to connect, but a scheduled, mechanical and goal-oriented event. Our marriage struggled as we went back and forth on whether or not to continue treatments, and my emotions took us both on a roller coaster ride I didn't know how to control. I cried a LOT and my body no longer felt like my own. It was a vessel for tests and needles and manipulation. Yet, I was determined to have a baby—no matter the cost, physically, emotionally, mentally, or financially. There were some very dark days—days when I literally looked at the world through blackness and a deep, aching sadness. Why me? Why us? Wasn't I good enough to be a mom? What did I do to deserve this? What lesson am I supposed to be learning in all of this? Whatever it was, it was completely lost to me in that moment.

In 2008, I was dumbfounded when the nurse told me I was pregnant after our "last hope" round of IVF (invitro-fertilization).

Life as I had dreamed it to be was finally happening.

I couldn't wait to get big, waddle around, buy baby clothes, and decorate a nursery.

I couldn't wait to welcome my baby to the world.

But the Universe had other plans.

At five-and-a-half months pregnant, I went into labour and gave birth to twins—Isaac and Lily. Lily was our warrior. Isaac was our

Chapter 9
Becoming Unshakeable

wounded. Lily was stable and strong. Isaac struggled to survive, his tiny one-pound, five-ounce body connected to so many I.V.s and machines trying to keep him alive. The doctors did not hold out much hope for Isaac and, after many conversations, we decided to let Isaac decide. We took him off life support three days later.

Our parents came to be with us and say their goodbyes. We sat silently in the private family room in the Neonatal Intensive Care Unit (NICU), the sun already setting outside on the cold and bleak November evening and a chill hung in the air. We each held Isaac for the first and last time while the nurse manually pumped air into his tiny, frail lungs. You could have heard a pin drop in that room. It was quiet except for the soft pump of air being pushed into Isaac's lungs...in, out, in, out, in, out.

Telling the nurse to stop pumping was one of the hardest things I have ever done. I could barely get the words out through my tears. For thirty minutes afterward, my husband and I were alone with our son as the nurse stood silently by the door, giving us time to say our goodbyes. But how do you say goodbye to your child? We held him, told him that we loved him and that it was okay to go. When Isaac took his last breath, I felt his tiny body relax and we knew his fight was over. As the nurse gently took him from my arms, I felt like a piece of me was being ripped away. Our parents came back into the room, and I fell to the floor at my mother's feet and wept, not knowing if or when the tears would stop, eventually crying myself to sleep in her lap. Time lost all meaning and there was so much darkness. Isaac was dead. I had lost my son.

The only light in all of this was Lily. My warrior daughter struggling to stay alive in the next room. At only one pound, three ounces, Lily's fight was just beginning. I knew I needed to be there for her, to pour my love into her, to be her mother. I could not get lost in my grief over losing Isaac. I had to be strong for Lily.

I was a mom now.

From Darkness to Joy

When you lose a child, your child is never lost. They live on in your heart, no matter how broken it is.

My grief was so overwhelming and painful that I buried it and only let tiny, "manageable" pieces surface from time to time. I would cry into my pillow at night until I fell asleep, choosing to grieve alone so as not to upset others or make them feel uncomfortable. If a song came on the radio that touched my heart, I would be in tears driving down the highway, full body sobbing with snot running out of my nose, pulling myself back together before I arrived at my destination so no one had to witness my grief. When I looked at Lily, my heart would break into a million pieces knowing that she would never know the joy of having her brother here with her. Like the strong, brave woman I thought I had to be, I kept my grief to myself. I suffered alone. I didn't ask for what I needed because I didn't know what I needed. What I did know was that I had to put on my big girl panties and be a mom. So, I pulled on every ounce of strength I had to show up every day for Lily. To be the mom she needed and the mom she deserved. My grief could wait.

I was a ghost of the person I used to be, moving through my life like I was watching myself from a distance. Depression hedged on the outer edge of my sanity and sleep was fleeting. Anxiousness over Lily's survival predominated my every thought and remained with me for years. The idea that I would ever feel joy again—the joy that you feel in your bones, not just surface joy—was elusive.

Chapter 9
Becoming Unshakeable

How could I possibly feel real joy after losing my child?

As Lily grew, we would talk about Isaac being in heaven and imagined him playing hockey with my uncle and getting cuddles from my grandmothers. We would laugh about the things he might have done with us and then cry tears together as we mourned him. I thought that because I could now talk about Isaac more openly and not always cry when his name was mentioned that I had a handle on my grief, that I had "gotten over" it. That I was good.

But I was wrong.

Funny thing about grief…it sticks around until you take time to acknowledge it, feel it and release it. I learned this in a very profound way in 2021 when I was chosen to do a TEDx talk on that very topic.

I thought I was ready to talk about Isaac. But when I sat down to write my speech, the floodgate of emotions that had been waiting patiently under the surface burst forth and my tears started flowing. Writing opened up a part of me that I had locked away…my deepest sadness, my broken heart, my shattered dreams for Isaac and Lily, and the death-grip of fear that I harboured underneath everything—that I would lose Lily. All these emotions came crashing to the surface as I wrote, and I was afraid that I wouldn't be able to do my speech. I could barely get through reading it out loud without breaking down in tears. I still had SO much more grief to feel that I had been unaware of.

Writing about Isaac finally gave a voice to my deepest grief, and I couldn't stop writing. Crying and writing. Writing and crying. These are what my days were composed of. Writing became cathartic and I found myself yearning to write and cry and let it all out. When the day finally came for me to say my speech, I did. Without breaking down. Without tears. I was able to honour both Isaac and Lily that day.

Losing Isaac was not the only grief event I had experienced over my lifetime, and it won't be the last. I was bullied for five years as a child, leaving me with a debilitating sense of unworthiness and a deep-seated fear of rejection and judgement. I experienced deep heartache over the break-up with my first love. I lost one of my favorite uncles three months before I had the twins and both my grandmothers when I was in my twenties. My marriage ended in 2016 when we realized that we weren't happy together anymore. I lost jobs, a business, and friendships. I have been rejected and demeaned for holding beliefs different from those closest to me. My grief came in so many different packages. Each time something happened, the grief attached to it got added to my emotional storage bank and was pushed down and ignored, rather than faced and felt. For me, this build-up of unacknowledged grief started to show up as moodiness, easy to tears, quick to anger, high anxiety, insomnia, and some bad decisions. But I didn't put two and two together until I started writing, releasing my emotions, and then noticing how much better I felt. I was calmer, less angry, less anxious, slept better, and was making good decisions. I felt lighter and, surprisingly, happier.

Initially, I was afraid to release the sadness I felt over Isaac's death, afraid that if I didn't carry the heaviness of grief inside of me, I would forget him. But that is the furthest thing from the truth. By releasing my emotions, I made space to remember him with love, not just sadness.

Intentionally allowing the tears to come and giving myself permission to feel all the feelings that had been hiding for so long—

Chapter 9
Becoming Unshakeable

sadness, anger, despair, frustration, blame, guilt, relief, resentment, disappointment, shame—was a transformational moment for me. It helped me to start to take control of my grief. All the emotions built up inside of me were like a pressure cooker just waiting to let out steam. As soon as I opened the valve, out they all came. And the pressure was released. The catalyst was writing about Isaac, but the release of emotions was from decades of unacknowledged and unprocessed grief.

With this continued practice, I really started to feel joy again. Grief was no longer the underlying constant in my life. And when upsetting things happened, I was able to work through my emotions much easier and faster and return to a place of peace and joy. I was starting to become unshakeable...and a deeper purpose awoke inside of me.

I felt compelled to support other women through their grief journeys.

As women, we are wired to suffer in silence, to be brave and strong, not be a burden to others. But when grief happens, the healing comes from connection, not isolation. Connection to our emotions and connection to others.

My TEDx talk catapulted me into working in the grief field and fueled my passion to help and educate others. I became a regular contributor to two magazines, writing about grief. I created workshops about grief that both educated and supported women in healing. I started coaching women individually, using the tools that I had learned, and was profoundly moved as I consistently witnessed their healing and newfound joy. I started speaking on stages and shared what I had learned, with the hope that it would help just one other person.

I have been told that I am strong, and I do believe that to be true. But becoming unshakeable—a place where I could confidently handle whatever was thrown at me—required a depth of courage and vulnerability that I could not have done on my own. To all the women who supported me, guided me, and loved me, I thank you.

ABOUT THE AUTHOR: In 2008, Margaret faced the unbearable loss of her three-day-old son, twin to her daughter, Lily. This devastating experience plunged her into the depths of grief, where she confronted her deepest fears and unearthed layers of trauma. Within her pain, she discovered an unshakeable inner strength that ignited her life's purpose: to guide other women through their grief, freeing them from the chains of their past and allowing them to rediscover joy. Today, Margaret stands as the driving force behind EVOLV coaching, serving as CEO and Founder, a TEDx speaker, educator, writer, and Certified Dare2Declare© Vision Board Facilitator—all while indulging in her funky shoe addiction!

Margaret Dennis, Women's Life Empowerment & Grief Coach
EVOLV coaching
evolvcoaching.com
margaret@evolvcoaching.com
linkedin.com/in/margaretdennis

CHAPTER 10

Embracing Your Uniqueness

Sharon Loduca

When I reflect on my journey from a place of voicelessness and deep inner darkness to where I am today, I am definitely filled with a sense of pride. I am also somewhat alarmed by the power I surrendered and by how little I knew about the vast potential I carry within. This awareness has awakened me to both the shadow and the light within me. Both are breathtaking. Both are transforming. Both present themselves in every area of my life, each manifesting in very unique ways.

In order to unlock the untapped potential in my personal, social, and business lives—and appreciate the beauty therein—it was necessary for me to look at the people, places, beliefs, mindset, and decisions that were holding me back. Then there were the voices—oh, those darn, niggly voices that whispered doubts and sewed seeds of conformity. I had to sit with and understand how crippling and self-defeating the mindset can be. I had to acknowledge the weight of my own words and how I talked to myself—things like:

I'm not good enough, smart enough, or unique enough. I don't have anything original to contribute. What happens if I start a business and fail? I already buy my Fresh Fruit Juices from John Jingleheimer's Juicery around the corner. Aren't I just imitating him if I open my Pineapple Power Pucks outlet? Will I be sued for it? Am I a complete fraud???

We drive ourselves absolutely batty with overthinking. We don't believe we have anything to offer because we don't realize we are truly unique. But we are! We were born with unique thinking skills, unique mindsets, unique passions, unique intelligence, and a unique communication style. Each of us is uniquely hardwired in the way we live, love, and simply are. We each have an inner orchestra, ready to compose a beautiful symphony that is entirely our own. Imagine the liberation we would experience if we replaced "wrong" with "different" and let our paths diverge from our tribes' norms. Imagine allowing yourself the space to embrace the perfect, breathtaking, awesome, inspiring, refreshing, and unique gift that is YOU. That is truly at the heart of what makes us irreplaceable.

I decided to embark on a journey to find my own uniqueness and allow it to come to the surface—only to discover that it was never really lost. Neither is yours. It's right where it's always been since the beginning of (your) time. It's simply buried beneath layers of *stuff* that's gotten in the way. For me, that gift was buried under mountains of ash and rubble in various stages of rot and decay, reeking of death, loss, loneliness, and brokenness. It was buried so deep I thought that ash and rubble were who I actually was. The bad kid. The difficult one. The one who didn't have a voice. The one who must be beaten into submission. The one who couldn't do anything right. The one who didn't even know it was possible to have her own likes or dislikes. The absence of voice and the mandate to conform denied my very existence.

A simple act that sets my day's tone is an early-morning swim. I'm not competing in a marathon. I'm not even a good swimmer. Still, before I respond to the world, I take time to move and breathe and

Chapter 10
Embracing Your Uniqueness

just show up. This has crafted a rhythm to my days that is unique to me and my well-being. The pace of laps and the strokes in my swim are each a note in my personal symphony. Once I own this unique song that is all mine, it stirs me to be in tune with my creative flow. An ordinary swim transforms into a reflection of life's rhythms.

It's funny how different people bring out different sides of us and teach us how to dance best together in an effortless flow. I think of my three amazing kids and how I interact with each of them differently based on their personalities, their needs, and their way of receiving love, and I'm reminded that we literally build and live our lives based on every single interaction we have.

I once asked my mom if she noticed patterns or similarities among me and my eleven siblings. I wondered if, with so many kids, she had a well-oiled system for parenting. After all, by the twelfth child, you'd expect her to have a routine down pat. And she did run a tight ship, with a set daily schedule and a pristine home despite our one-and-a-half-year age gaps. Mom's response surprised me. She chuckled and said, "No two were alike. Every pregnancy, birth, and personality was distinct. All twelve of you are truly unique individuals."

This blew my mind. With so many of us, you'd think there'd be common traits, behaviours, or skills, but she saw us each as exceptional. She even mused that if she had twelve more (a daunting thought), each would also be distinct. Now, after a lifetime of working and interacting with people, I see that she was right; I see that the one consistent pattern among people is their uniqueness. I see it in my family, in my clients, when I coach other agents, in my most inner circle and my widest circle. There is in each person a uniqueness. Every. Single. One.

Now, let me bring this into my business—building, running,

developing, and expanding it. How do I rearrange the orchestra of my life to write a new song and reach a new, improved objective? How can I set myself apart from the others? You see, I'm a real estate agent and there are over 70,000 real estate agents in The GTA. That's a massive number. Just go sell a house. Sign here. Done. That's what most people believe. Yes, there are systems in place that we can (and should) use without reinventing the wheel, but that wheel doesn't wholly define me. It's one tool in my life to promote efficiency and allows me time and space to let my own unique, authentic creativity flow. This is where "brand" develops.

In order to set myself apart, I don't need to deny my own creativity or imitate anyone else. I learn from others. I observe what works and what doesn't work. I study changes and how they affect our industry. Then I look at the "why" in what I do and add that to the mix. I take the pieces that feed my "why" and sit with them to see how it all works together. The industry tools + my mindset + my skillset + my why = MY business model. With this math, you can see the industry tools are potentially a quarter of my business model—even though we are all "doing real estate."

David Goggins, a retired Navy SEAL and renowned endurance athlete, emphasizes performing at your peak even in challenging times. Embracing your unique self doesn't require perfect conditions; it's a conscious decision to silence doubt and embrace your voice, leading to discovering your path step by step on your journey. Sometimes your best is just showing up for you. There will absolutely be times when just showing up is more than you can handle. Show up anyway. As you stake your claim by showing up, things shift in your universe, and the impossible makes way for the possible. Your mindset changes, pushing the impossible to the sidelines, giving you moments of opportunity to walk in the fullness of what is, or

Chapter 10
Embracing Your Uniqueness

will be, possible.

The disconnect from our uniqueness is huge for many of us. We call this disconnection discomfort, restlessness, feeling lost, confused, depressed, empty, sad, internally bruised, and broken. And rightly so! The greatest transformation that happens in life is returning to your birthright, to your gift of uniqueness, to everything that makes you YOU. When I learned to shut out all those other voices and reject others' expectations, I began to return home to myself. I willingly let go of what anyone else thought. I learned to rest. The striving lessened. The anxiety calmed. I found my quiet place inside me. This was not necessarily an easy or short process. But, oh, what a darling process it is! Letting the light shine in all my broken places was a beautiful process of embracing my flaws and finding joy. Through this, self-love grew, humour emerged, and positive changes were made, including letting go of things that didn't align. The transformation happened quietly, even if unnoticed by others. As I embraced my true and unique self, I found wholeness and gained confidence. This transformation led to freedom, innocence, and personal growth. My life transformed as I became my authentic self. A new rhythm and balance emerged, letting my uniqueness shine.

Do I still strategize, overthink, and stress a little? Sure! But I don't stay there. We will never escape this life unscathed. We will experience all those painful places, but it is in how we walk (or crawl, or fly) through them, that we find our freedom. I am now free to be me. I am free to find my joy, celebrate my life, and provide for me and my family. I am free to learn and grow. I am free to be successful and to prosper in all areas of my life. In the midst of this journey, I will not be afraid of the dark and painful valleys that must be travelled. I will walk them, and I will grow through them.

This is as true for my business life as it is for my personal life. It's all interchangeable and transferable.

Now, let's go back to those voices that tell us we're not good enough. Nine people could be cheering us on, telling us how awesome we are. Then that one person comes along with some negativity, and—bam!—we hold onto that like it's the ultimate truth. We give it way more power than it deserves. But guess what? Today, I'm throwing out a challenge. Let's flip the script on that nonsense. Just you and me, rebelling against that pattern. Shut down that negative voice and crank up the volume on the positive ones. Embrace the love and encouragement from those nine voices. You do that, and you're on your way to growing into the incredible person you're meant to be.

It's not just others who bring us down, though; we do it to ourselves too. But guess what? We hold the power to change that. Start giving yourself pep talks, read affirmations out loud, and fill your mind with positivity. And hey, if you're struggling to find one person to give you encouragement, let me step in. You, my friend, are uniquely gifted and strategically positioned to fully live your life as it was meant to be lived. Yes, YOU! There is more joy ahead for you than you even know how to handle right now. Seriously, you've got more peace, love, and laughter coming your way than you can imagine. Amazing friends and success are lining up for you. Believe me, where your focus goes, growth happens. So shift that focus, and watch your life bloom! No one else has power over you unless you give it to them. I speak from an abundance of experience when I say that what you focus on grows. That is a universal law.

The success I chase in my business is tightly linked to my personal success. It's an inner game, and so is self-sabotage. Remember, you're the one holding the reins on which inner game you're playing.

Chapter 10
Embracing Your Uniqueness

While tools, coaches, and support are crucial for business growth, I've found that when I prioritize personal growth and let my true self shine, business challenges become way more manageable—things just click with less struggle.

Here's your empowerment tip: YOU get to CHOOSE which inside job you want! We can and should surround ourselves with those that get us and speak our language. There has to be a connection for the best results. But when you apply dedication and focus to your life—and endorse the inside job that allows your authentic self to dominate—the challenges, both personal and professional, become much less of an uphill battle. The journey is revolutionary. Transformational. It all reflects YOU. Consistently. Beautifully. Uniquely. YOU. The melody of your life, conducted by your inner orchestra, remains uniquely yours, and it's ready to compose a beautiful symphony that is entirely our own.

ABOUT THE AUTHOR: Meet Sharon, an unstoppable force of nature, published author twice over, and a dedicated mom. Sharon cherishes life by bonding with her three kids, a couple of crazy cats, and of course, Chase the Chihuahua. Sharon is also a seasoned Realtor, SRES Specialist, and Mortgage Specialist, skilled at turning your home dreams into reality. Her secret? Building genuine relationships and understanding her clients' needs. Sharon's achievements in Real Estate have earned her numerous well-deserved awards. Whether selling homes or indulging her passions for hiking, food, photography, and writing, Sharon has a knack for turning daily life and business into an adventure!

Sharon Loduca
SharonLoduca.com
Shar@SharonLoduca.com
647-880-6546

CHAPTER 11

Who Am I?

Kellie Haehnel

We are all guilty of letting life take control. I once prided myself on being a master juggler, able to keep all professional and personal balls in the air. I had a calendar that mapped out each event and activity to ensure that we didn't have to be in two places at one time. That calendar was truly a work of art, and necessary to keep our very busy lives running smoothly.

I worked fifty-plus-hour weeks as an HR Manager; my husband was a corporate executive and traveled for his job occasionally during the work week. Our older daughter, who was twelve at the time, was a competitive figure skater and had to be at the ice rink by 6:00 a.m.—not to mention the weekend skating competitions. Both girls spent several nights a week at dance classes, and were active in Brownies and Girl Scouts. Weekends were for getting caught up on laundry and housework. We were blessed with a new home, the opportunity to take wonderful vacations to Disney World and cruises, and—I thought—a very fulfilling life.

Then, that life changed on a dime. Within one week, I got laid off from my job, I served my husband with divorce papers, and I took my daughters and moved in with my sister (unfortunately, on the younger daughter's eighth birthday). As if that wasn't enough, I found myself without access to our family funds (in other words—I had no money)...and I was about to turn forty! There is a list somewhere of the most stressful life events—and in that week I experienced most of them.

I took two days to do the non-productive pity party. Then, I sat up and asked myself, "Who am I?" I could no longer identify myself as an HR professional (at least not one currently employed), and soon I would no longer be a wife. I no longer identified as someone who enjoyed a beautiful home and wonderful vacations, or had money. I could still call myself a mom...but who was I *as a person?* I couldn't answer the question; in fact, I suddenly felt as if I had no direction or purpose in my life.

Yet the question sparked several realizations. I had been moving through the demands of day-to-day life—merely surviving, not thriving. I had been focused on the kids, not myself or my marriage. I also discovered that perhaps the busyness was my way of avoiding looking at areas of my life that weren't working. I had created a false sense of control, and had been focusing on the material things instead of what really mattered. Was this the life I wanted for my children? I wasn't sure, but I knew there had to be more to life than this!

My mind then traveled back to when I was fifteen years old. My father was killed in a trucking accident, leaving my mom, at age 43, to raise three teenagers alone. I was so proud of the strength she displayed, creating an environment where we felt safe, loved, and provided for. Six months after Dad's death, she followed her intuition and went back to school to fulfill her lifelong dream of being a registered nurse—and she graduated with all A's! She had a wonderful career that provided her purpose and security through the rest of her life. Thinking about the new life she had built inspired me to do the same. Though our situations were different, her example gave me the strength to move on.

I started spending time with myself...talk about uncomfortable

Chapter 11
Who Am I?

silence! I took walks, and when I was able to, I would go to the movies by myself (bonus: I didn't have to share my popcorn!) or even take myself out for a solo dinner. Eating dinner by myself was certainly an exercise in vulnerability—I felt everyone would stare at me and say, "That poor lady, she has no one." I didn't feel I had any value; I didn't feel wanted. Sure, I was surrounded by supportive family and friends, and while I was very grateful for them, I couldn't escape the fact that I no longer had a job or a husband. Amazing how much importance I placed on those things as a source of my identity and worth.

Six weeks later, the Universe threw me a bone—a big one. My girls and I were able to move back into our home, and my soon-to-be ex-husband was court-ordered to make the mortgage payment. I was then hired to create an HR department for an up-and-coming IT company. Though it was a cut in pay, I took it as more evidence that the Universe truly did have my back.

Of course, there were still hurdles to navigate. A short six months after I accepted the position, the company closed. I was unemployed once again! Then, a year after we moved back into the house, we got the court order to sell it. Where was I going to move without a job! That same night, I found a new listing for a lovely townhouse right in our school district. I got in the car and drove over. There was no for sale sign, but a gentleman was standing in the driveway. I inquired about the listing, and as luck would have it, he was the realtor. He showed me the townhouse and I just knew it was mine. I didn't know how, but I just knew.

The next day, I met with my financial planner, who encouraged me to put in an offer with a ninety-day contingency. I looked at him and laughed! I had been unemployed, on and off, for a year, and the housing market was struggling. He reminded me that the house was in an excellent school district and how, with my HR experience, I would have a job. It took a leap of faith, for sure, but I took it and put in the offer…which was accepted! Now all I had to do was sell my house and get a job within three months. It was a tall order, but I told myself, "I can do this!"

I kept telling myself this, even as October 31, our deadline, drew closer, with no progress.

"You need to get centered," a friend said to me one day.

My reply: "You think?!"

She then invited me to a Reiki session. I had no idea what Reiki was, and after she explained it to me, I decided to give it a try. I was spinning with no direction, so what did I have to lose? After the session, I felt more at peace and that I was perhaps standing on firmer ground. She then encouraged me to really explore who I was at my core—to focus, not on who I was in the past, but on what I wanted to create going forward. She reminded me that I had a blank page, a new chapter in my life story that I alone got to write. How empowering! She also left me with advice that changed everything: to ask my soul what steps I need to take to bring my life into being.

As I spent time with that question, I realized she was right: I didn't have to define my future by my past. I could let go of the fear and instead **F**ace **E**verything **A**nd **R**ise! I had the strength, tenacity, and abilities needed to create a new and amazing life. Like my mom, I could set an example for my daughters so they realized they were worthy of doing whatever they dreamed of doing and that they deserved to be seen, heard, and respected.

I got busy working on developing a positive mindset and taking small steps daily to rebuild my life. Soon after, in the middle of September, we got an offer on the house, and they wanted to close at the end of October! Calling it close, don't you think, Universe? Okay, now all I needed was the job, which I was offered a week before we were to close! The catch: the job would begin on November 4

Chapter 11
Who Am I?

(remember, I had to close on the house and the townhouse by October 31!) The Universe sure has a wicked sense of humor! But through it all, I kept the faith and trusted that it would all work out, not realizing that I was taking the first steps of a life-changing journey.

I also continued with the Reiki sessions, leading to such profound experiences that I had to learn more about it. I am now a Reiki Master Teacher, Integrated Energy Therapy Master, a Life Force Energy Master, a Level III Medical Intuitive, a Life Purpose Coach, and a Jack Canfield Success Principles Train-the-Trainer. I will be forever grateful that my first Reiki experience opened a whole new path for me!

I learned tools that aided me in embracing my authentic self. These tools were valuable and an important first step to putting myself first. I discovered what true self-love is all about. To never underestimate the power of self-love. Many people think that self-love means being selfish, and so they often overlook its importance. But the reality is that self-love is one of the key ingredients to your mental well-being. It doesn't mean being selfish, it just means not being too tough on yourself. Self-love is a vital aspect of personal growth and well-being. I feel it was about accepting and valuing myself for who I am and treating myself with kindness and compassion.

If you can't love yourself for what you are, you can't love others either. You need to change the way you talk to yourself, so stop the negative self-talk. You need to appreciate yourself, rather than continuously "cursing" yourself and your luck each time a problem shows up in your life. This is not about engaging in destructive patterns of behavior and turning a blind eye. It has nothing to do with arrogance or narcissism and everything to do with becoming a fully whole and integrated individual.

When you can exercise self-love, your life will become so much easier. I started embracing the fact that I was worthy just as I was;

as a mother, a woman, and a professional, I stopped self-sabotaging. I realized I created much more stability in my life when I no longer depended on others for fulfillment or validation. This gave me a sense of being grounded and more peaceful.

Some of the tools I use daily in my life and teach in my classes and retreats include meditation, visualization, journaling, understanding our life path colors, and soul-inspired discussions—to name a few. I live each day with gratitude and am happier than I have ever been! These tools have helped me move through cancer and other health issues, job layoffs, and other life challenges with ease. They have also sparked more gratitude for my fulfilling HR career, and assisted me in inspiring my coaching and energy-healing clients. Most importantly, I see my daughters, who are now grown and successful in their own lives, utilizing these same tools!

We can't always control what life throws at us, but we can control how we react to life challenges. In my Success Principles Training, I learned $E + R = O$, which stands for: the Event plus your Reaction creates the Outcome. We all need to take personal accountability for our reactions and the outcomes we experience. Each reaction is a choice. Do you choose to be a victim or a victor?

Again, it is about creating a positive mindset and coming back to our core values. When we are centered and anchored in our authentic selves, we have the strength and tenacity to face anything with grace. Knowing that the Universe has our back. Trusting the journey. Searching for gifts in each and every experience—even the challenging ones. Those gifts grant us the ability to reflect and realize how much we have grown and guide us on which path to take toward our vision of the life we wish to create. There are signs everywhere!

I couldn't see the gifts in those experiences during that tumultuous week, but I certainly do now. The greatest of those gifts: discovering

Chapter 11
Who Am I?

ME and my calling to inspire others to redefine their purpose, reconnect with themselves so they learn to put themselves first, and gain clarity on their vision. To let them know that they are not on this journey alone. To be that lighthouse guiding them from the stormy sea of their lives to the safety of the shore. Aiding them in navigating the difficulties so they can create and write their next chapter. Offering them compassion, understanding, and a steady unwavering presence when they need it most.

It is important to reach out to for ask and accept help. The Universe puts people and teachers in our path to aid us in moving through life's challenges and experience profound transformation and triumph in our own lives. We all deserve it—especially YOU!

Live Life Inspired by Awakening Your Soul™

ABOUT THE AUTHOR: Kellie Haehnel is a life coach who aids high-achieving women in navigating changes in their lives—be it career, empty nest, divorce, finding their purpose, and so on. She is also a Reiki Master, Integrated Energy Therapy Master, LifeForce Master, Level III Medical Intuitive, Certified Life Purpose Coach, and a Jack Canfield Success Principles Train the Trainer. She also provides Intuitive Toe Readings and retreats/workshops. Kellie explores thought-provoking methods with loving support in a safe, heart-centered space where her clients feel guided, gain clarity, and are open to all the possibilities of living the life they desire.

Kellie Haehnel
The Spirit Wellness Center
thespiritwellnesscenter.com
kellie@thespiritwellnesscenter.com
612-804-4463

CHAPTER 12

Through the Fear
Cliff-Diving for Beginners
Heaven Sofia

*"There is only one thing on this earth
more powerful than evil, and that's us."
~ Buffy the Vampire Slayer*

I would not describe myself as fearless. When I was a teenager, most of my friends spent their summers and weekends adventuring. I had a job and usually worked nights and weekends. While everyone else was enjoying adolescent shenanigans and developing core memories, I was serving burgers and scooping ice cream. Sometimes my friends would visit during my shift and I would get to hear about all their wild adventures. I was envious, but I knew it was because I wanted to be included too. One day, I heard them talk about a local cliff they'd been diving from. I was amazed and terrified at once. My friends must have sensed my eager curiosity, because on my next day off I found myself riding to the cliff with them.

Sometimes, when making plans, I don't think what I'm planning will happen. I usually expect people to cancel or a conflict to arise. The same was true back then, so I didn't believe we were actually going to jump off a twenty-foot cliff into a lake—which, to my horror, turned out to be a large pond—until we reached our location. Once we reached the top, a debate began as to who would jump first.

Nervous and expressing concern about the water depth and visible tree branches in the water, I knew one thing: I wasn't jumping first. I didn't even know if I could jump at all. I was not a cliff-diver. I was the person who always had a stomachache and jumped at her own shadow. One of my friends pitied me and said, "It's fine, Heaven, we know how you are. Go ahead and walk back. We'll see you at the bottom."

I didn't need to be told twice.

Alone at the bottom, I carefully stepped into the water. I swam a little, then floated on my back to watch my friends.

One by one, they jumped. No one else gave up the way I did. I was so impressed by them, and a little sad that I didn't do it. I wanted to feel what it felt like to go over the cliff, take that leap into the unknown, and do something terrifying.

I didn't know if I would ever take an opportunity to do something like that and experience that sensation…until six years later, when I went from a victim of abuse to an activist lobbying for a cyber civil rights law.

When I was a teenager, I had a stalker who socially isolated me until I dated him. What many people perceived as unrequited young love on his part and a messy, coercive teenage relationship ended with me being the victim of nonconsensual pornography, also known as "revenge porn" and more accurately referred to as Image-Based Sexual Abuse (IBSA).

IBSA was a nightmare that defined my self-esteem, relationships, and even my career. IBSA could have destroyed me, yet it is why I know what it feels like to dive headfirst into unknown territory.

In 2010, I began receiving emails from men on Craigslist

Chapter 12
Through the Fear

responding to a solicitation ad that I had supposedly posted. It only escalated from there. My abuser set up dating profiles and social media profiles. Then it went beyond him. People were catfished using my pictures, believing that they were in a relationship with me. I started to get threats to my physical safety and messages wishing me harm.

You're a whore, not a woman.

It's not the worst thing that's been said to me, but for some reason, this sentence replays in my mind every time I share this part of my story. It is a straightforward statement, but adequate for the intended purpose. Does it mean anything to me anymore? Not really...So why do I still remember?

In college, I went to law enforcement. It's ironic to me now, all these years later. I went to them for help, but as I continued to advocate for myself and others, they learned to come to me for help. They didn't know how to handle it then, and very few are educated on how to handle it now.

Back then, I was directed to two different police stations, and neither could decide which was supposed to help me. Instead, they had me file a report with the FBI. Nothing came of it. I called lawmakers, attorneys, and women's rights groups. Still nothing. I went to my abuser's university and escalated my complaint. I finally had a little hope because, as far as I knew, he was still a student. The VP of Student Affairs tried to help me, but they couldn't do anything because he had dropped out. There was no institutional recourse to be found.

Some of the people I went to in search of a solution turned around and asked me for help because they'd had a similar experience themselves. They had never told anyone. I had been collecting resources, so even in my directionless, depressed, about-to-give-up-on-life-itself state, I had more information than they did. Unfortunately, I also learned that some people, when they can't help you, will find a way to blame you instead.

Thankfully, I found an incredible attorney named Elisa D'Amico, who was a co-founder of the Cyber Civil Rights Legal Project. She introduced me to the Cyber Civil Rights Initiative, and some terms they use describing technology-facilitated sexual abuse, including:

- Image-Based Sexual Abuse (IBSA)
- Non-Consensual Distribution of Intimate Images (NDII)
- Synthetic NDII
- Sextortion
- Child sexual exploitation/abuse material (CSEM or CSAM)

Elisa coached me through what to do and how to handle the harassment. But legally, she couldn't do anything for me. She wasn't licensed in the state of Oklahoma, and there wasn't even a law in place to protect victims.

Eventually, my family and friends started receiving messages. I didn't have a choice but to tell them what had been happening to me as it now affected them. I had to tell them. Not law enforcement, not the student success center…my friends and family. Even though I told a few people, it wasn't until after graduating that many more found out because I needed to tell them.

I *had* just started my first career after graduating college, and, like most young and excited people do, I updated all my social media—which I believed I had set to private. I received some messages of congratulations, but I also received another message. A disturbing one. It was definitely not the first or even the worst—like I said, this had been happening for years, and if I was listed on any website for an organization or job, I inevitably received messages or was

Chapter 12
Through the Fear

threatened with blackmail. But for some reason, the way they did it on that day, right after I had been so excited about my new job, it pissed me off more than it frightened me. I think that's the day my fear broke. I'm still a human, and I still experience fear, but now it's not something that makes me freeze. It's something that makes me want to understand and conquer it.

I used to reply to these messages but my attorney advised me to stop, so I did. I stopped. The massive, organized, and anonymous community who had been virtually harassing me, sharing screenshots, and celebrating when I responded to them, started to complain amongst themselves that I was no longer engaging with them. They wanted a reaction, one that I simply would not give—not to threats, compliments, or other baits. Many lost interest because I became, frankly, boring to harass. Some members of that community thought that my silence was an opportunity. Unfortunately for them, I did too.

My dad is a retired journalist, and he always told me there were no shortcuts. The only way through something *is to go through it*. It wasn't the advice I wanted, but probably the advice I needed. Because of his career, he had seen what cyberbullying was doing to youth and young adults. I think this made him the perfect father to have during this type of crisis. The support was unreal.

When I asked my parents if I could partner with a journalist to get this story out there, he said he knew just the one: Maureen. She helped me get through it.

Maureen was the investigative journalist who fought to get me in the right rooms with lawmakers to tell my story. Her reporting, her empowerment, and her friendship gave me the strength and the courage to do something I never thought I could do: go public.

Maureen and her photographer, Dre, interviewed me, lawmakers, and my family, who really put themselves out there. My dad, who was on TV five days a week but never talked about his daughter now did so, and my mother, one of the shyest people you'll ever meet, put herself out there too. It sent a message. Having that backup and support sent a message. That's the power of community. My community became so vast. I found people and people found me. Professors and administrators from my university came out and made statements about what I had gone through and supported me. I was shocked.

In 2016, SB1257 criminalizing NDII passed, and in May the governor signed the bill and gave me an original copy.

My first time jumping off that cliff into the water wasn't going to a journalist or being on TV. It wasn't going to the state capital and asking strangers to listen to me. It was small things that added up over time: talking to my friends, my university, telling my family, leaving unanswered voicemails to lawmakers, sitting in a room alone with various male police officers who had no idea how to handle what was happening, and ultimately getting sent away with no resources.

It was waking up every day and choosing to keep going. I still joined the organizations I was interested in—quietly, but I still did it. I got a new job, but wouldn't post about it on LinkedIn. I still went to the grocery store, because even if my harassers knew exactly where I lived, and likely, where I shopped, I still needed to eat. I couldn't stop my life out of fear.

I really did my best to try and choose a quiet life. I fought owning this for a while. We can't control much in this lifetime, but one thing we should have ownership over is our image. Our bodies. They belong to the person inhabiting them. And for some reason, we aren't born with those rights. In certain situations, we have to file for copyright to have legal ownership over our images. Is it up

Chapter 12
Through the Fear

to lawmakers who owns the rights to our images and who owns what we can do with our bodies?

In this era where our digital lives are our personal lives, the issue of consent is more critical than ever. We must assert our ownership over our images and bodies. Our bodily autonomy is under constant threat in so many ways. There are people who want to tell us what we can do with our bodies. People who wish violence against these temples we inhabit. Respect is so much easier on the soul, but many choose judgment and hate.

I don't harbor hate for those who hurt me; I don't harbor love for them either, that's not my brand. I pity them. They'll never know what it's like to step out of their own shadows. In the time they spent messaging me and calling me names, researching me, contacting my employers, my friends, and my family for the purpose of dehumanizing, extorting, and silencing me (and many others), they could have spent that time working on their own lives, and the fact that they didn't is really sad.

I want to challenge you to be brave every day, to do one bold thing every week, and experience something truly courageous at least once in your lifetime. Leap into the unknown.

It's liberating. Truly. Own the narrative. Be scared, do it anyway. Dive in. I did, so I know you can too. I am an adult who sleeps with a nightlight. I have weird dreams sometimes that take me back to that cliff and there is an ominous presence there. It wants to stop me from conquering my fear. I wake up so scared I don't want to open my eyes. When that happens I say aloud, " You've got ten seconds to get out before I rain hell on you!" I think that sums up my personality, though. I will make it through the fear.

Please don't live in shame. Ask for help. Build your community. Easier said than done, but the one I have now was ten years in the making. Find your people. Do something bold. Change the freaking world because you can.

I thought stepping into ownership of my story, my body, and my worth would help me forget. Surprisingly, the memories are part of what makes me stronger, the memories that serve as time capsules benchmarking my transformation. The journey and struggle to push beyond all limits and redefine the meaning of power will never end...at least that's what they said on *Dragon Ball Z.*

ABOUT THE AUTHOR: Heaven Sofia is a healer, bodily autonomy advocate, research assistant, and small business owner. After experiencing the harmful effects of cyberbullying and Non-consensual Distribution of Intimate Images (NDII) firsthand, she decided to advocate in her home state for legislation criminalizing the act. She has consulted with survivors and law enforcement and continues her work in empowering others through one-on-one coaching and remaining vocal in driving change that protects vulnerable populations.

Heaven Sofia Taylor
Social media: @heavensofiatea
HeavenSofiaTea.com
HeavenSofiaTea@gmail.com
facebook.com/HeavenSofiaTea

CHAPTER 13

A Cause for Pause

Cindy Rose Ferguson

I have been abused, betrayed, abandoned, and greatly blessed in this life. I am grateful for each moment of this journey, and what a journey it has been.

My early years were marred by unspeakable abuse and trauma, followed later by life-threatening illnesses and soul-wrenching losses. All these experiences have and continue to serve and guide my path, giving me opportunities to learn and understand more of this human condition. I continued to survive and even thrive, that is…until I didn't.

Forty years of awaking to the "get up just one more time" mantra that had kept me showing up abruptly changed one morning. It just felt different, like I didn't have one more ounce of "get up and go" left in me. I was wrong.

There are times it may feel that life is offering more challenges than we are able to bear. Have you ever asked yourself, "Why bother trying, when happiness can be squashed in an instant?"

Allow me to share some snippets of various years and stages of my life.

One morning, the comfort and the security of life as I knew it was shattered into a million pieces again; the black veil of hopelessness was showing up. Am I cursed or blessed? I chose to learn how to recognize the blessings, to take responsibility for how I feel, and rely on my ability to create peace in my soul. I had to learn how to forgive myself so I could forgive and release events and moments from a loving, peaceful soul. Thankfully I did learn this.

I was in a fulfilling career with a leading international company in my industry. After twenty years of smaller operations in this industry, I was finally part of something much larger, with endless opportunities for growth.

The year following this exciting time brought the sudden death of my soulmate. This was not my first experience with the loss of security and love I had come to trust. In reflection, I was able to find peace and acceptance to carry on.

I had a major motor vehicle accident two years later that would challenge my mobility for the rest of my life. Those mobility issues, coupled with the effects of the head injury, led me to begin to understand the brain in greater detail so I could better understand my "new" self.

My brilliant and accomplished mother ended her life the same year as my motor vehicle accident. She was only fifty-three, and had endured many years of misdiagnosed mental health issues, including severe bipolar disorder.

I prayed for a year's reprieve after all of this so I could catch my breath and pull my spirit back together. It had taken many years to cultivate my Rosie Outlook and it was starting to wane; I felt it.

My prayer was answered, and I was gifted one of the best years of my life. I found the daring to dream again of a future, with a partner, travelling the world, building an amazing career, socializing,

Chapter 13
A Cause for Pause

entertaining and having fun—living out loud, if you will!

Then, one lovely, early spring day, I rounded the corner at the bottom of the stairs in our home to look up and see my partner hanging lifeless from the rafters in the recreation room we were creating.

Just ninety minutes earlier we had made plans for the day as we listened to the song "La Vida Loca." We had a list! We laughed as I did a little dance to the song. We had plans.

This can't be real.

The horror and the shock were palpable. My body felt like it had been thrown into the cold concrete wall, then I felt an icy grip from head to toe, followed by a searing fire throughout my body. I wasn't strong enough to get him down. I was gasping for air and composure. I ran to dial 911, then back downstairs to him to try again to release him from the hanging posture, then next door to get family to help.

The finality was real; he was gone. In the ninety minutes I had taken to shower, get ready for the day, and briefly visit my office to attend to some business, he had taken his life, and as a result life as I knew it was about to change drastically…AGAIN.

The chaos and agony only got worse! I became the brunt of the family's grief. They didn't understand his passing and his choice. I was bullied, manhandled, threatened and accused of murder by the same loving family members that had embraced me the day before. I was numb, stunned, and broken down into a crumbling mass of flesh.

That was twenty-four-years ago, almost to the day, as I write this.

In the story of my life, it has become another "Day Other Than Today."

It may have been yesterday or a yesterday fifty years ago. It could have been a day of great joy or a day of tragedy. The dates and events are etched in my soul, in my being at a cellular level. As years turn into decades and decades into milestones, we collect many *"days other than today,"* and they all serve in the journey of becoming the person we are currently, in this moment.

To this day, my body and soul experience the trauma of that day and its aftermath. I am reminded to take a moment to honor that feeling and replace it with Grace. Gratitude for the challenge has been found because the events and circumstances compelled my soul to seek greater understanding and become a voice to those in need.

I am not here to tell you life is a bed of roses or to "fake it 'til you make it."

I'm here to tell you that with each and every moment we exist, we have the right of choice.

I'm here to tell you the greatest healing of all is in self-awareness and accepting your life with love, for, after all, you are loved.

I'm here to tell you that life is a commitment to self-worth and forgiveness for others and yourself. This is a valiant, often painful journey while navigating the many challenges of survival that can lead to the loving harmony of the life you seek.

We can learn how to cope in order to function day to day. This is called survival. Having peace in your soul and love in your heart is living.

When we become aware that our body and soul are in Dis-Ease and begging for peace, the Universe (God, Spirit) will respond in many ways. We need to be open in order to become aware of the many signs and gifts that come our way. I believe acknowledging them with gratitude is also paramount.

Chapter 13
A Cause for Pause

We have so many opportunities to learn, grow, and find the clarity and tools to help us persevere what is being brought to us through our circumstances. Strangers who appear out of nowhere and create light for us, along with books or articles we happen to notice and resonate with, are just a few examples. Even through illness, loss, and trauma there are little steppingstones of experience leading to knowledge and better understanding.

Then we must step into the difficult yet the most loving task of all: acting upon the knowledge, the coaching, the signs, and the blessings and bring that sense of balance into our life. We need to be learning and unlearning habitual responses. We need to be learning and re-learning empowering actions and mantras used in the past and embracing ones that can move us forward. When others are part of the experiences and journey, I find comfort in the phrase, "To thine own self be true."

Decades ago, I came across a Confucius quote that stuck with me and has proven valid throughout my life: "When the student is ready, the teacher will appear."

Now, over five decades into the often tumultuous process of releasing what no longer serves me to develop an awareness of my role in creating the life I live, I can come from a place of love and grace. Do I still experience paralyzing fear and severe depression at times? Absolutely! However, I work hard to draw on the countless life lessons and coping tools I have learned. I'll keep getting up one more time to rise above my own limitations because I am aware of my ability to do so. Life helped me prove this—to myself. I choose to believe in me, to seek knowledge of myself and humankind, that it may shed a seed of awareness that may take root and grow.

The pages of my life are many and still being written.

This chapter, riddled with suicides, illnesses, and an accident, speaks briefly of a few detours in my path that led me to "a cause for pause" in my life. If this cause for pause were to bring awareness to even one reader, that we may rise above even the most difficult challenges, then my time has been well spent.

My life went from very active businesswoman and community member into total darkness in a minute of time. The darkness lingered and it took many years to stumble my way back out.

Decades of working to rise above childhood trauma, deal with adolescent fear that led to rage, and my partner's suicide has given me ample opportunity to seek knowledge and develop a loving balance in my life. I had to find this balance and knowledge.

In reflecting—there I was at forty, confident that the struggle was over; I could feel safe and secure, pursue my dreams, fulfill my purpose. I had survived it all and kept my faith and courage throughout. Then the beautiful bridge I'd built creating my peace on earth went crashing down. I found myself drowning in the darkness.

My internal survival biology took over and kept me numb; my brain shut down to protect my soul and I self-isolated for years. I didn't want people to see me because of the grey aura that shrouded me. Every self-doubt and feeling of failure re-emerged to weaken my being. This was not my character historically and caused great concern for my loved ones.

I sought professional guidance through counseling, therapy, and medicine. For many years I maintained a level existence of daily function. It was not what I would call living. There was no creative thought or joy, simply existence.

A powerful message, imprinted on me when I was around ten years old and facing upheaval, has stuck with me through all of

Chapter 13
A Cause for Pause

this. I was leaving the safety of the province I grew up in, and the reassurance of having my Nanny close by, to move three provinces away. These were my Nanny's words to comfort my fear and sadness: "Cindy, you can be anything you choose, stay loving, stay kind, believe in yourself and don't let anyone shit on you." I took that to heart and remind myself often of the many blessings that came from some of my darkest hours of my life. I'd rather reflect on those blessings than giving my energy to the sadness or loss. Like any new belief or habit, it will take practice and grace to learn how to be kind to yourself.

I will end by telling you that this is your life and only you can create your reality through your thoughts and actions. The circumstances of how we got to today had their purpose. To hold onto the anger, the fear, and/or blame the past for our life today will damage the body and soul.

Let go of the "right" or "wrong." Gift yourself the time to get to know you. Honor yourself. Give yourself the grace to become aware of the role we play in all our interactions. Give yourself the grace to become aware of the role we play in our outcomes. Acknowledge the blessings associated with every challenge survived and accept that only you can change how you feel about the challenges.

I'm honoured to share I have been actively participating in life since 2017 (six years ago at the time of this publication). That same year, I had a horrible fall that destroyed my left ankle and led to four days in hospital, reconstructive surgery, three months of non-weight bearing, and the list goes on. I had choices in attitude and what my life could and would look like. I saw a marketing commercial to become an Avon Representative and I answered it. I made a choice to show up. I have been in the top sales category since the beginning.

I have reduced my weight by fifty-five of the nearly hundred pounds I had added to my five-foot-one frame through the events of my life. I have joined with other business and products that align with my beliefs and purpose and I am grateful.

A cause for pause—sometimes this is a gift, provided for us to stop, look, listen, and then move forward.

ABOUT THE AUTHOR: Cindy Rose Ferguson maintains a rosey outlook on life knowing she is blessed and shielded by Angels. A veteran businesswoman and spiritual warrior, Cindy has survived and thrived through repeated traumas throughout her life, including childhood abuse, the death of two husbands, a divorce, her mother's suicide, a major accident that limited her mobility, four major surgeries, three miscarriages, and infertility. Primarily her belief is we have a purpose, seeing every challenge as an opportunity to learn. After a twenty-year "detour" from life, Cindy's spark has returned, a radiant glow of holding Light for others.

Cindy Rose Ferguson
cindy@acauseforpause.ca
acauseforpause.ca
facebook.com/groups/acausefopause
705-818-1563

CHAPTER 14

Surviving to Thriving in Life!
A Transformational Journey
Christine L. Barlet

*I*n 2019, I came to the conclusion that I needed to take action and make a change in my life. I had been going down a path of self-destruction for several years—thanks to a combination of perfectionism and working under chronic stress, along with menopause, fibromyalgia, anxiety, depression, and—most importantly—having no idea of who I really was. I realized I was living inauthentically and confused about my purpose, which had led to unhappiness and struggles with self-love and acceptance. I had prioritized my life around others' wants and needs and sought fulfillment through caring for them and making sure everyone was happy. I needed to feel needed in order to feel valued. Little did I realize that I was creating more damage than being of actual service. I was a strong-headed, determined, self-motivated, and unstoppable woman who always had her shit together—at least I thought so until life knocked me on my ass, ran me over with a tractor trailer, and then backed up and ran me over again! I was deflated, defeated, and lost—mentally, physically, and spiritually.

It was as if I was having an out-of-body experience. Thoughts of unworthiness and being judged constantly ran through my mind. Each morning I would wake up, look in the mirror, and question myself: Who are you? Why are you here? Where did that young, vibrant, force of nature go? I had been drafted to an internal war that I was not prepared for. This internal battle and feeling of being lost became my new normal. I found solitude in isolation and comfort in eating dark chocolate and ice cream. My health, wellbeing, and marriage was spiraling out of control, and I had no clue how to stop it. I was plagued by uncertainty, fear, self-doubt, and indecisiveness. I was in survival mode—lost in what felt like an abyss, a place I'd never even fathomed existed. To sum it up, I had hit ROCK BOTTOM!

I spent the next several months playing tug-of-war with my thoughts and emotions and praying for clarity or a sign on which direction I should go. Instead, I got intrusive thoughts. I stopped doing the things that I loved such as eating healthy, working out, and spending time with family. I lost my passion for life and willpower to carry on. I attempted to bury the ugly truth about what I was going through so I could be there for my family, all the while thinking, *This can't get any worse.*

I had a routine visit scheduled with my family doctor and decided this is my last chance and only hope to get help before it was too late. The night before my appointment I made a list of all my symptoms and mustered up the courage to put the list in my purse so I could go over it with my doctor the next day. However, as I sat beside my husband in the doctor's office, I began to feel sick to my stomach. My body was in fight-or-flight mode and my mind was racing with thoughts of the disappointment and frustration I was certain my husband would feel when he heard all of this for the first time.

The appointment began like any other: the doctor entered the room, gathered basic information, reviewed test results and went over my list of current medications. He then began asking the standard questions pertaining to mental health. I paused, feeling my face turning red, my heart racing, and my anxiety heightening. This

Chapter 14
Surviving to Thriving in Life!

was it—my window of opportunity! Take it! I could barely keep myself composed. As I unraveled my list and began to read off the symptoms that I was experiencing I could feel my husband's gaze and shift in energy. The doctor and I continued to go through a Q & A session. I thought to myself, *You're doing great. Remain strong and keep your shit together!* Until I was asked the one question that broke me. The question that needed an honest answer. The doctor asked, "Do you ever feel like the world would be a better place without you?" I paused again, not because I wasn't sure of my answer because I wasn't sure whether my husband was ready to hear the truth.

"Yes," I said finally, adding that I felt like the world would be a better place without me and my family would no longer have to bear my burdens. I looked at my husband, he looked at me, and a flood of emotions took over. I felt relieved and fearful at the same time.

This was where my journey of self-discovery and transformation truly began. My path to authenticity, self-love, and gratitude. A newfound appreciation for all of my life's trials and tribulations as pieces of the puzzle that led me to living with purpose and inner peace. A life filled with clarity and excitement. An opportunity for exploration and being able to have a meaningful impact on other women. I was at a pivotal moment in my life. Decisions had to be made and a new journey arose from such darkness. I made a difficult but necessary decision to resign from my senior leadership position that I worked so diligently to obtain and had been so passionate about for almost twenty years. After resigning, I took two years off to take time to heal mentally, physically, and spiritually. It was time for me to do me!

Of course, putting myself first was unchartered territory. I traveled a lot around the U.S. and did a lot of reading and soul-searching. I was also blessed with the opportunity to be an involved first-time grandmother and partner up in business. Two years flew by, and

I felt I was ready to start the next chapter of my life. During this time of exploration, I had finally figured out what I wanted to be when I grew up. I was relieved and elated! I wanted women to know that there is hope and that they are not alone. The importance of trusting in the process. I wanted to collaborate with women by creating supportive and empowering relationships to guide them on their journey to optimal health and wellness.

I took the leap of faith and enrolled in school to become a National Board-Certified Holistic Health and Wellness Coach for women. This journey was transformational—Mind, Body and Soul! I have always been passionate about heath, wellness, and empowering women to be the best version of themselves. I am now able to live with purpose, be authentic, and connect with women who are like-minded and share similar life experiences.

While on this journey I faced a fork in road—one with the potential to impact my future or make a decision to dwell in the past. Only I can make the decision to persevere or remain at a standstill. This journey ignited a growth mindsct. Mistakes became life lessons and opportunity for growth. A new way of living where self-care and inner peace is at the forefront. Where my strengths, values, abilities, imperfections, and commitment are appreciated. The feeling of hope that I had once lost found its way back into my heart. The climb to the top of the mountain was now within my view. I was equipped for whatever obstacles or barriers that life wanted to throw my way. The journey was an uphill climb, but it was necessary for self-discovery. Once I reached the top of the mountain, the breeze was slightly cool against my skin and the setting sun was warm on my face. I stood there and exhaled, all while reminiscing of the old version of me. The version of me who had lost herself to depression, being overly critical and unkind to herself and her needs. I now embrace this woman by expressing gratitude and empathy. As without her, there would be no me. This

Chapter 14
Surviving to Thriving in Life!

has been an amazing transformational journey which has led me to an amazing revelation where everything makes sense and is in alignment. My purpose in life is now clear. I am here to serve through pure intentions and to be true to what makes me happy.

As I stand there in silence overlooking the path that I have traveled and admiring how far I have come on my journey. I give myself grace and remind myself that I am still a work in progress, or shall I say, a masterpiece in the making! My journey has just begun, and I am now equipped with the tools and resources that I need to keep on thriving and doing meaningful work. My life is no longer controlled by the fears of being judged, the fear of failure, or the drive for perfection. I have just begun to restore balance and a sense of feeling connected holistically—mentally, physically, and spiritually. I am no longer just surviving I am actually living and thriving in life!

ABOUT THE AUTHOR: Christine is the founder of Surviving to Thriving Holistic Wellness LLC. She is a Women's Holistic Health & Wellness Coach and Certified Holistic Nutrition Specialist. After years of personal experience dealing with burnout disorder, compassion fatigue, and hormonal imbalances she decided to embark on a new journey into health and wellness. Today, her passion and purpose in life is to support women who are feeling disconnected and imbalanced and have a desire to live authentically. Christine empowers women to take control of their health and wellbeing through an integrative approach dedicated to the mind, body, and soul for optimal health and wellness.

Christine L. Barlet
Surviving to Thriving Holistic Wellness LLC
survivingtothrivingholisticwellness.com
survivingtothrivingwellness@gmail.com
484-706-9520

CHAPTER 15

Thriving
One Day at a Time
Jaclyn Kane

So many people ask me why health and wellness has become such an important part of my life. Well, if you have a little time, I'll tell you my story.

I am a "Jersey Girl," through and through. I grew up in Central New Jersey by the Jersey Shore; I went to schools in the Middletown, New Jersey school district and graduated from Middletown South. The plan was to go to community college; however, I soon realized it wasn't for me. I wanted to be making money.

I had been working since I was about fourteen, but my first real full-time job was in Belmar at a ticket broker's office. We sold tickets for Broadway shows, concerts, and all sorts of events. It was a small office and I made wonderful friends I still keep in touch with to this day. Though I worked there for a while and made some pretty good money, I knew this wasn't a lifelong career. I would have to look in New York City for something, but I wasn't sure what that was. At that time, there were still industries where you could work your way up the ladder, even without a college degree. A headhunter set me up with several interviews at brokerage houses, most of which don't even exist anymore. After several weeks of going into the city to interview, in the summer of 2000 I landed a position at Aon

Financial Services Group located at 2 World Trade Center. I wanted to shout, "Look at me! I'm twenty years old and I work in THAT BUILDING on the hundredth floor!"

At Aon I made decent money, but, even better, I made some best friends, the closest of whom was Michele Reed. Michele and I always had a blast. We were inseparable at work and even signed up for a gym membership at Lucille Roberts, where we took cardio kickboxing every day during lunch. In our free time, we did a couple of things with our boyfriends. We really built a beautiful friendship.

Even my commute to Manhattan turned out to be fun. Each morning I would take NJ Transit from Red Bank to Newark and switch to the PATH train that would take me directly into the World Trade Center. One morning I ran into Dave, an old high school friend, who was also working downtown. Dave and I had so much fun laughing and doing stupid things on our commute that time flew by and we'd be in the city before we knew it.

On September 11, 2001, I woke up to a perfect day, with bright sunshine and cool fall weather. I put on a black V-neck shirt, khaki pants, and black platform shoes. As I was leaving the house, my mom said something she never had before: "You look really nice today!" Little did we know it was an outfit I would remember forever.

Dave and I met on the PATH train for our daily commute. As usual, we were laughing and not paying attention, but at some point we started to notice that a lot of people were exiting the train at stops in Jersey City. This was odd, as the World Trade Center was the last stop and everyone got off like a herd of cattle. We dismissed it at the time, and when we pulled into the WTC and smelled smoke we just thought it was a track fire, as that happened often with newspapers and things like that. When we exited the train, we walked to the escalators to go up to mall inside the WTC and noticed that the escalators were pretty empty for a Tuesday morning. When we

Chapter 15
Thriving

reached the top of the escalator I said, "Later, Loser!" and Dave and I parted ways to go to our offices. After taking just a few steps toward 2 WTC, I noticed that the entrance was blocked off by the FDNY and NYPD. Clearly, something wasn't right. I turned around, saw Dave, and started screaming for him to wait for me. Finally, he heard me and stopped to wait.

That was when everything changed. Dave and I saw the fear in everyone's eyes. We were walking over body parts and were seeing things falling from the sky. We didn't know what was going on and were ushered across the street by NYPD and FDNY so we would be safe from whatever was going on.

We stood on the corner and looked up, as everyone was. People were chattering in the background, "It was an accident! A helicopter accidentally flew into the building! How horrible of an accident this is!" We stood there and watched people desperately trying to scale down the WTC from the upper floors. No one made it. All I could think was that everyone from my building must surely be evacuating down the stairs and that they'd be safe. And that's when it happened. I heard a SWOOOOSSSHHH and BOOM! When I looked up, I saw that American flight 175 had crashed into my building. We stood and everything was silent. Everything was happening in slow motion. For whatever reason some man pulled me into the phonebooth with him to protect me from the glass and debris falling from the sky. And protect me, he did. Right where I was standing, part of the plane's wing landed and could have cut off my legs, or worse.

Chaos ensued, and Dave and I got split up in the crowds running for their lives. The thoughts in my head were so elementary. *Must run. Must go. Must get far. This building is going to collapse. I don't want to be here.* I ran in those high platform shoes to the Blarney Stone, a bar on 34th Street, in about forty-five minutes. Crazy what adrenaline will do to you. I walked in and found an area at the bar (it was PACKED), ordered a shot of Jameson and then proceeded to watch my building collapse on TV. Now all I could think about was Michele. Had she made it out? Where was she? Why wasn't she answering her cell phone?! Why was it going to voicemail?

NYC went on lockdown, with all forms of transportation into and out of the city at a standstill. The tunnels were closed, but I had made some friends that day and we stuck together. I had called my mom several times during the day for updates, and about four o'clock she finally said that the ferries were running and to get over to the East Side to catch one. My feet were raw and blistered, but I was determined to get out. I caught one of the last ferries leaving. I finally made it home and had an emotional reunion with my family. But still nothing about Michele.

A few days went by and my department had a conference call, where they would say people's names to see if they were okay. To hear the dead air when many names were called was heartbreaking. Michele was one of those names.

Determined to find something out about her, my boyfriend and I started going to the Red Cross tents in the city almost every day. I can still smell the smell of the toxins burning out and around the WTC site. It's a smell I will never forget. After several weeks we gave up and hoped that some DNA would match hers and we could have some closure, but Michele was never found. My company lost one hundred seventy-eight people that day, most were never recovered. I pray for them all the time.

Life eventually went on, but it was different now. I suffered from extreme anxiety and PTSD, and still do. The nightmares and flashbacks were a part of daily life, but I trudged through the days, the minutes, and sometimes even seconds. This became my new normal, and though they don't come as often anymore, I still live

Chapter 15
Thriving

with these scars daily. But I survived, right?

Not so fast!

Flashforward to March 2017. I was now living in Bergen County, New Jersey with a few girls. One morning I was in the shower and felt a lump in my breast. It felt really big but I thought nothing about it. A couple days later I felt it again and had my roommate feel it. She felt it too and I became alarmed. I called my mom, who said it was probably a cyst (breast cancer doesn't run in our family), but that Monday I made an appointment with my doctor who told me to go and have a mammogram to check it out. She seemed concerned so I went directly to the Breast Center at Holy Name Hospital and waited until they could get me in. Several hours later, I was finally called back. After the test the nurse came in and said the doctor needed to speak to me. That's never a good sign and I was all by myself looking up at those stupid clouds they have on the ceiling. How is that calming? Anyway, he came in and said that it looked suspicious and he wanted to order a biopsy. That week went so fast and on March 17, 2017, I got the call to come into the hospital and was told that I had aggressive breast cancer and I needed to see an oncologist asap. I was like, *WTF!? I survived 9/11 and now this.*

Treatment started about two weeks after I saw the oncologist. My tumor was five-and-a-half centimeters—or almost two inches—which was big. I would have the chemotherapy, a bilateral mastectomy, and radiation. We had all come to realize that this was a 9/11 cancer (I tested negative for the BRCA gene) from all the toxins I had breathed in that day and the days after when I was going back in to search for Michele. They didn't get me in 2001, but it sure came to bite me in my ass several years later.

During chemo, they were giving me steroids to keep my weight up and it sure did—to the tune of a fifty-pound weight! I'm not a big person so this was a lot for my frame.

When I was finally cleared to start exercising again, I started to look into science-based diets that would help me lose the weight and hopefully keep the cancer from coming back. I basically started to coach myself, writing affirmations, hiring a personal trainer, and staying motivated. The pounds came off pretty quickly and stayed off; I was probably in the best shape of my life.

Since I had done this myself, I started to look into a career in health coaching. If I could do it, certainly others could do it with motivation and accountability. I started my education at Dr. Sears Wellness Institute in 2021 and became a Certified Health Coach. After that I decided to take the Master Certified Health Coach course and am now sitting for the National Board of Health and Wellness Coaches this year. Given my history of trauma—in addition to 9/11 and breast cancer, I also survived child abuse and domestic violence—I felt called to practice in the Trauma-Informed Coaching arena. My goal is to help people cope with their trauma using techniques to guide them to live their best lives in the present day. Trauma is not a disorder, but an adaptation, and we can live full lives, every day, thriving one day at a time.

ABOUT THE AUTHOR: Jaclyn Kane, a Master Certified Health Coach and Certified Trauma Informed Coach, dedicated her life to dispelling the stigma surrounding trauma as a mental disorder, recognizing its profound impact on recovery. A survivor of child abuse, 9/11, domestic abuse, and breast cancer, Jaclyn connected deeply with fellow survivors, fostering empathy and healing. In 2021, she earned her diploma from the Dr. Sears Wellness Institute. Hailing from Central New Jersey near the Jersey Shore, she settled in South Florida alongside her loyal companion, Cooper. Jaclyn's earthly journey ended in August 2023, but she continues to shine on through her legacy.

About the Authors

**Are you inspired by the stories in this book?
Let the authors know.**

See the contact information at the end of each chapter and reach out to them.

They'd love to hear from you!

Author Rights & Disclaimer

Each author in this book retains the copyright and all inherent rights to their individual chapter. Their stories are printed herein with each author's permission.

Each author is responsible for the individual opinions expressed through their words. Powerful You! Publishing bears no responsibility for the content of the stories by these authors.

Acknowledgements & Gratitude

We could have reached out to each contributing author in this compilation and asked, "Who do you wish to acknowledge and pay tribute to?" We are confident they would have provided us with a long list of family members, companions, friends, and mentors who had played a role in their lives and stories. Rightfully so, for no one gets there alone.

If you asked "us" as the ones who were instrumental in pulling these individuals together for this book, we would without doubt share that "community" is what needs to be acknowledged. By this we mean the coming together of many diverse people with varied backgrounds and experiences with the common goal of sharing a moment of time that impacted them, changed them, and that they hope will ripple out and change others. YOU are one of the others.

We wish to acknowledge you. Read these bravely expressed words within. Know that they were written for you. You are worthy, you are valuable, and you matter. Everyone has their story, but nobody gets there alone, and we are here for you.

About Cheryl. A. Clark

"It's not the choices we make that define us, it's the reasons for making those choices." Author unknown.

Let's face it, we all judge a book by its cover. We live in a fast-paced world where we seldom take the time to ask questions, let alone wait for answers. We have been taught to view many instances, situations, and appearances through a certain lens that we merely adopted – not through one we own and crafted.

Cheryl A. Clark had to remove her lenses. She had to take what she had been taught, what she had adopted based on peers and consensus and remove it all in a 295-day detainment – it frankly was a matter of survival.

Now you will find Cheryl helping others craft their own "lenses" through empowering people like you to share your steps, share what may have LED you to this, this moment.

Cheryl A. Clark owns LED ME TO THIS, a platform growing and becoming a voice for those taking steps we may not understand. It is a platform of acceptance. A platform of non-judgement. You are not your choices.

Have a story to share? Reach out to Cheryl A. Clark. Want to be inspired? Find Cheryl and others sharing at www.ledmetothis.com

LED ME TO THIS
ledmetothis.com
mystory@ledmetothis.com
facebook.com/ledmetothis

About Jamie Allen Bishop

Wife. Mom. Entrepreneur.
Author. Speaker. Explorer.

Some fun words Jamie uses to describe herself. With a background in spirituality, leadership, and education, Jamie has learned a lot over the last 30 years about growing a business from the ground up.

Entrepreneurs are amazing people! They have a heart for creating something special, pursuing a purpose, and making a happy business venture their reality. And Jamie wants happiness for everyone!

Since mindset impacts financial success, Jamie helps her clients shape their attitudes, behaviors, and responses to the opportunities and challenges they encounter. If life isn't already a dream come true, our mindset is what needs to shift.

Jamie believes that having a growth mindset can set her clients up to achieve their ideal lifestyle faster and easier than they may believe. Albert Einstein is coined with saying, "The definition of insanity is doing the same thing over and over again but expecting different results." Jamie helps break the cycle of what no longer serves her clients to catapult them into alignment with what is already theirs. In a nutshell, Jamie helps her clients to take their businesses to the next level of success.

In the words of Mahatma Gandhi, "If you want the world to change, start with yourself."

Jamie Allen Bishop
Mindset Coach for New Entrepreneurs
jamieallenbishop.com
jamie@jamieallenbishop.com

About Clare Bennett

Clare Bennett, hails from Bonnie Scotland, with core values of love and authenticity. Her own life purpose was birthed through a dark night of the soul, and having come through the other side, she now helps guide others on their life path.

With a treasured collection of certifications in Life Coaching, Meditation, Reiki, NLP, Clinical Hypnotherapy, Psychological Astrology and Therapeutic Tarot, she aims to be a beacon of support and guidance for those seeking purpose and emotional well-being.

At her Glasgow-based sanctuary, Temple Divine, Clare draws inspiration from her own transformative journey to help others find and love their inner selves. Her mission is to support people to empower themselves. Clare helps people embrace their life's purpose, take care of their mental and emotional well-being, and cultivate meaningful love with themselves and others.

In addition to her professional expertise, Clare is deeply committed to fostering a sense of community and believes in the power of raising each other up. Her deep belief in the capacity of individuals to heal and reveal their authentic selves is the cornerstone of her work. Clare Bennett's compelling narrative is one of resilience, growth, and love.

clarebennett.scot
connect@clarebennett.scot
facebook.com/templedivineglasgow

Powerful You! Publishing

Sharing Wisdom ~ Shining Light

Are You Called to Be an Author?

If you're like most people, you may find the prospect of writing a book daunting. Where to begin? How to proceed? No worries! We're here to help.

Whether you choose to contribute to an anthology or write your own book, we're here for you. We'll be your guiding light, professional consultant, and enthusiastic supporter. If you see yourself as an author partnering with a publishing company that has your best interest at heart and expertise to back it up, we'd be honored to be your publisher.

We provide personalized guidance through the writing and editing process, as well as many necessary tools for your success as an author. We offer complete publishing packages and our service is designed for a personal and optimal author experience.

We are committed to helping individuals express their voice and shine their light into the world. Are you ready to start your journey as an author? Do it with Powerful You! Publishing.

Powerful You! Publishing
239-280-0111
powerfulyoupublishing.com

Collaboration Books

Empowering Transformations for Women
Women Living Consciously
Journey to Joy
Pathways to Vibrant Health & Well-Being
Women Living Consciously Book II
Healthy, Abundant, and Wise
Keys to Conscious Business Growth
The Gifts of Grace & Gratitude
Heal Thy Self
Empower Your Life
Heart & Soul
The Beauty of Authenticity
WOKE
The Art and Truth of Transformation for Women
Women Living On Purpose
U Empath You
Women Living In Alignment
Heart Whispers

Allow Your TRANSFORMATION to be Your TRIUMPH.

The Destination is the Journey.

Made in the USA
Middletown, DE
14 December 2023

45600867R00080